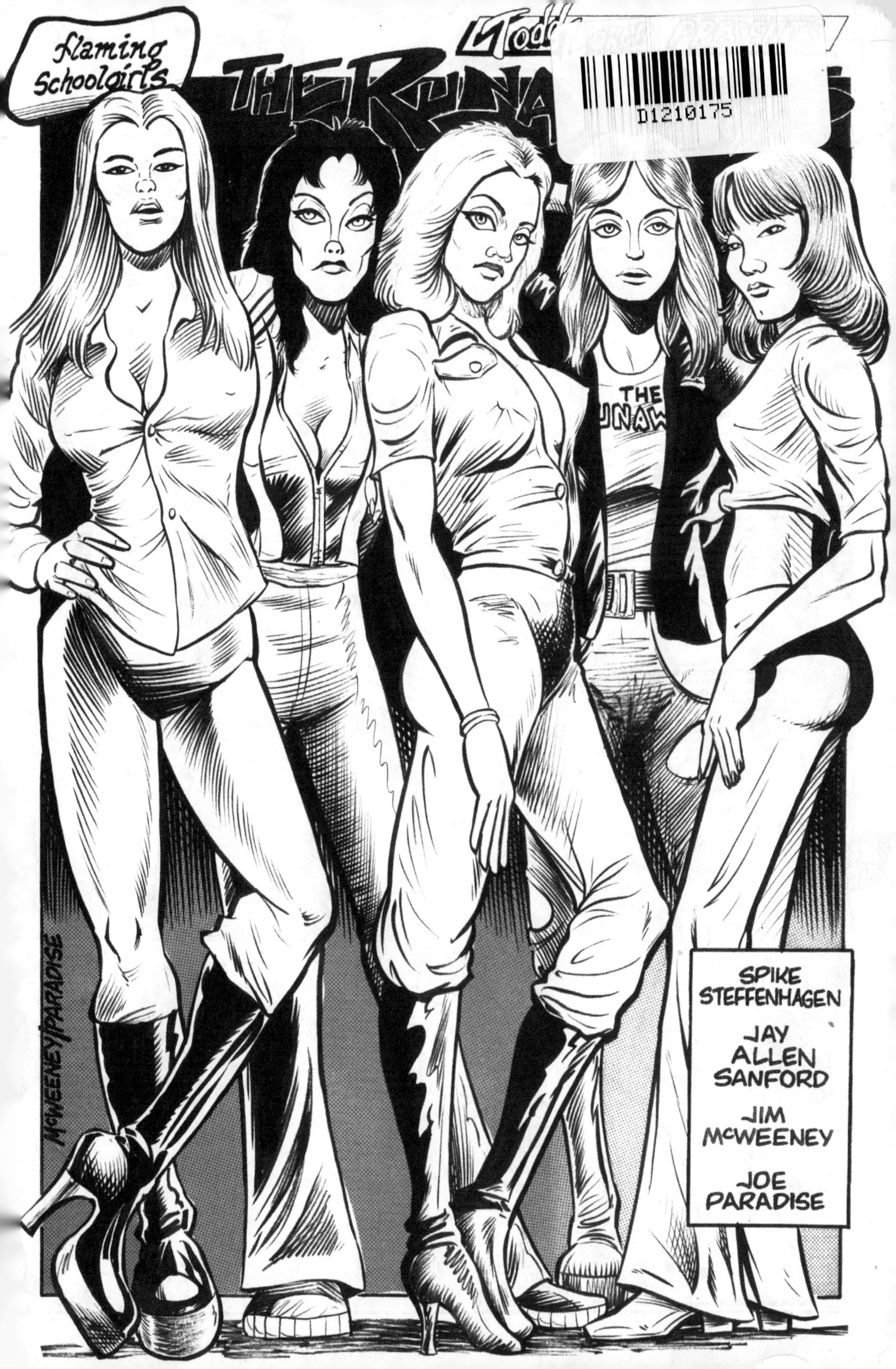
Flaming Schoolgirls
Todd
THE RUNA
D1210175
THE
McWEENEY/PARADISE
SPIKE STEFFENHAGEN
JAY ALLEN SANFORD
JIM McWEENEY
JOE PARADISE

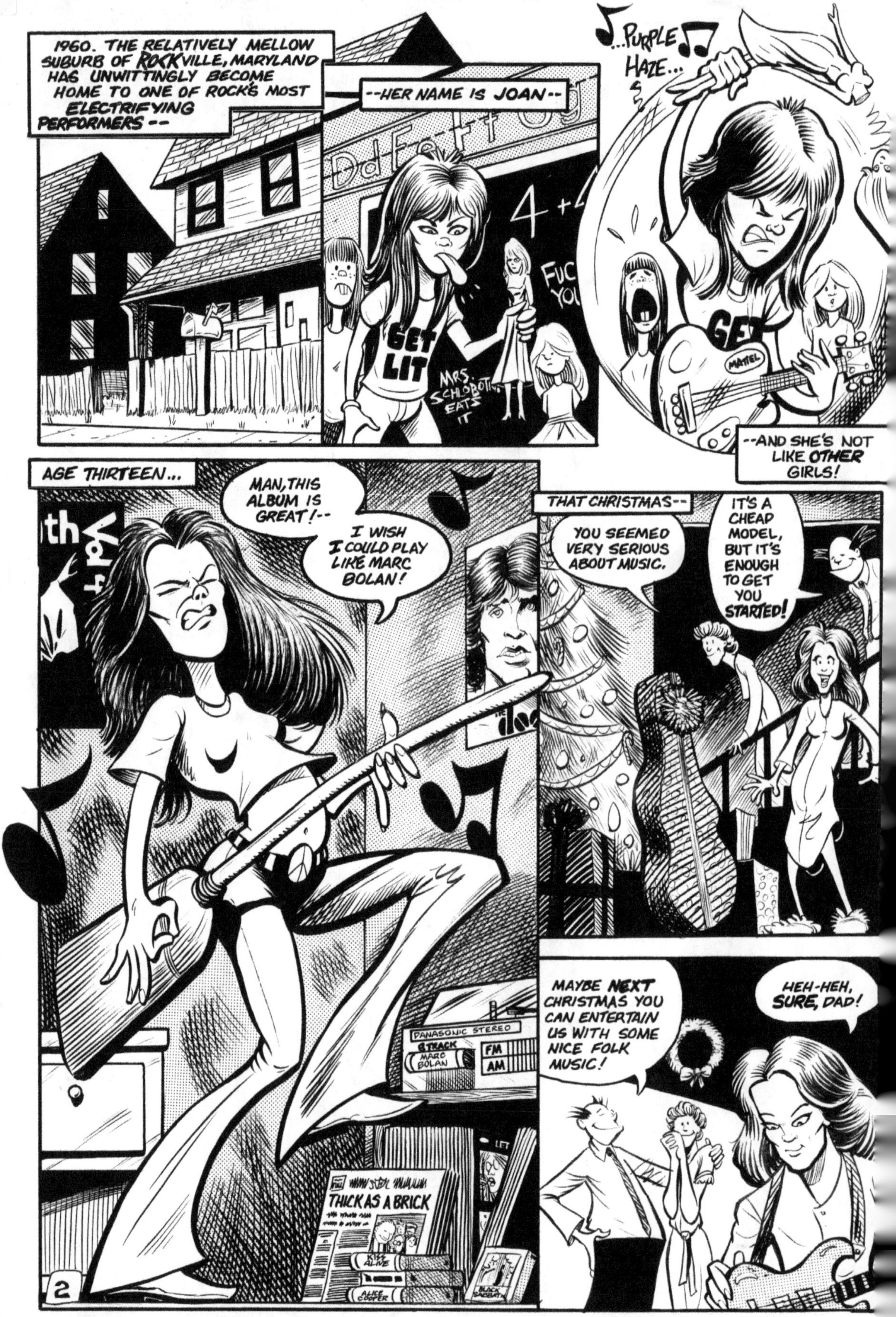
1960. THE RELATIVELY MELLOW SUBURB OF ROCKVILLE, MARYLAND HAS UNWITTINGLY BECOME HOME TO ONE OF ROCK'S MOST ELECTRIFYING PERFORMERS --
--HER NAME IS JOAN--
GET LIT
MRS. SCHLOBOTT EATS IT
FUCK YOU
...PURPLE HAZE...
GET
MATTEL
--AND SHE'S NOT LIKE OTHER GIRLS!
AGE THIRTEEN...
MAN, THIS ALBUM IS GREAT!--
I WISH I COULD PLAY LIKE MARC BOLAN!
PANASONIC STEREO
8 TRACK
MARC BOLAN
FM
AM
THICK AS A BRICK
KISS ALIVE
ALICE COOPER
BLACK SABBATH
THAT CHRISTMAS--
YOU SEEMED VERY SERIOUS ABOUT MUSIC.
IT'S A CHEAP MODEL, BUT IT'S ENOUGH TO GET YOU STARTED!
MAYBE NEXT CHRISTMAS YOU CAN ENTERTAIN US WITH SOME NICE FOLK MUSIC!
HEH-HEH, SURE, DAD!

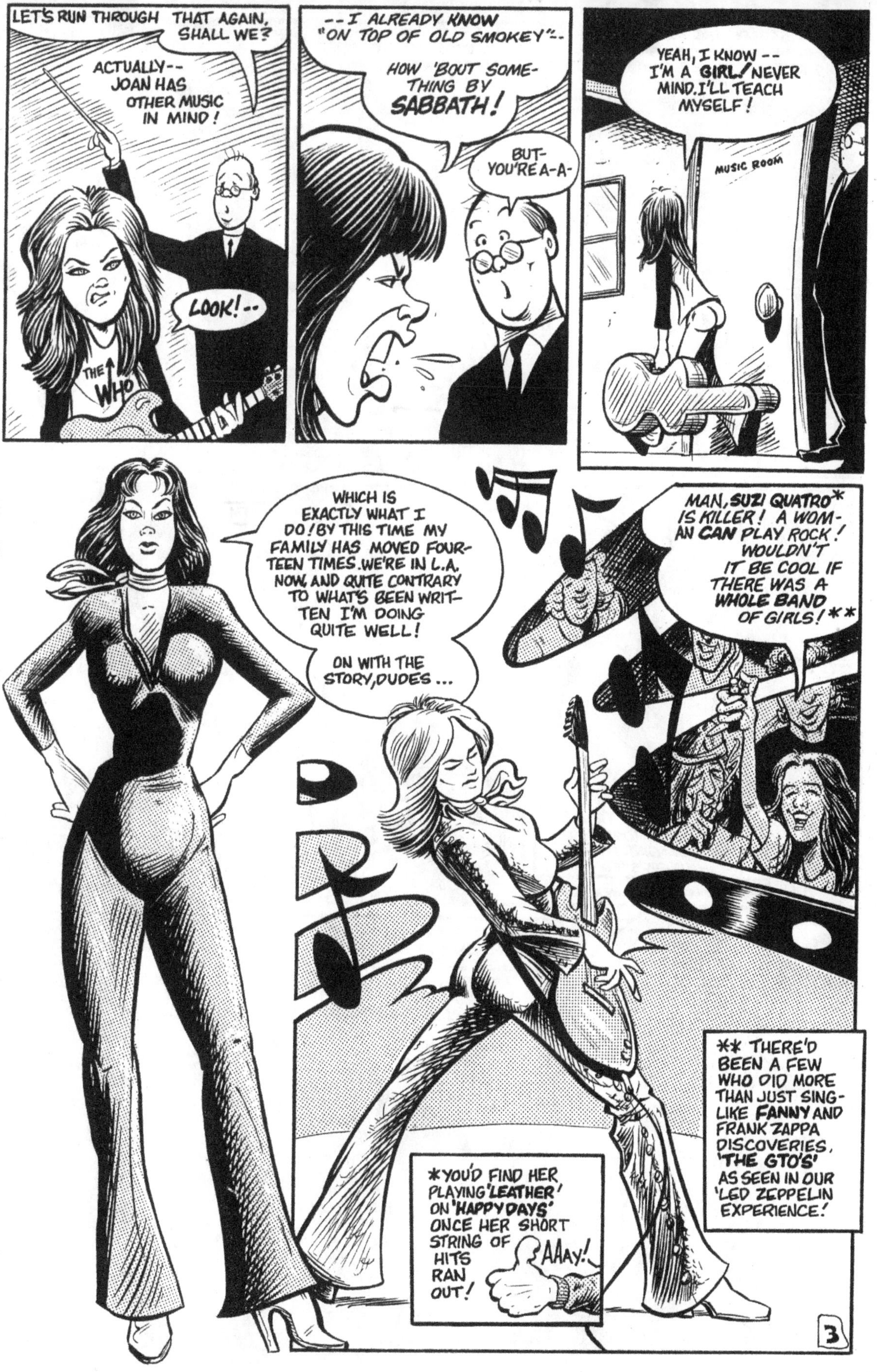
LET'S RUN THROUGH THAT AGAIN, SHALL WE?
ACTUALLY-- JOAN HAS OTHER MUSIC IN MIND!
LOOK!--
THE WHO
--I ALREADY KNOW "ON TOP OF OLD SMOKEY"--
HOW 'BOUT SOMETHING BY SABBATH!
BUT- YOU'RE A-A-
YEAH, I KNOW -- I'M A GIRL! NEVER MIND. I'LL TEACH MYSELF!
MUSIC ROOM
WHICH IS EXACTLY WHAT I DO! BY THIS TIME MY FAMILY HAS MOVED FOURTEEN TIMES. WE'RE IN L.A. NOW, AND QUITE CONTRARY TO WHAT'S BEEN WRITTEN I'M DOING QUITE WELL!
ON WITH THE STORY, DUDES ...
MAN, SUZI QUATRO* IS KILLER! A WOMAN CAN PLAY ROCK! WOULDN'T IT BE COOL IF THERE WAS A WHOLE BAND OF GIRLS! **
** THERE'D BEEN A FEW WHO DID MORE THAN JUST SING-LIKE FANNY AND FRANK ZAPPA DISCOVERIES, 'THE GTO'S' AS SEEN IN OUR 'LED ZEPPELIN EXPERIENCE!'
*YOU'D FIND HER PLAYING 'LEATHER' ON 'HAPPY DAYS' ONCE HER SHORT STRING OF HITS RAN OUT!
AAAY!
3

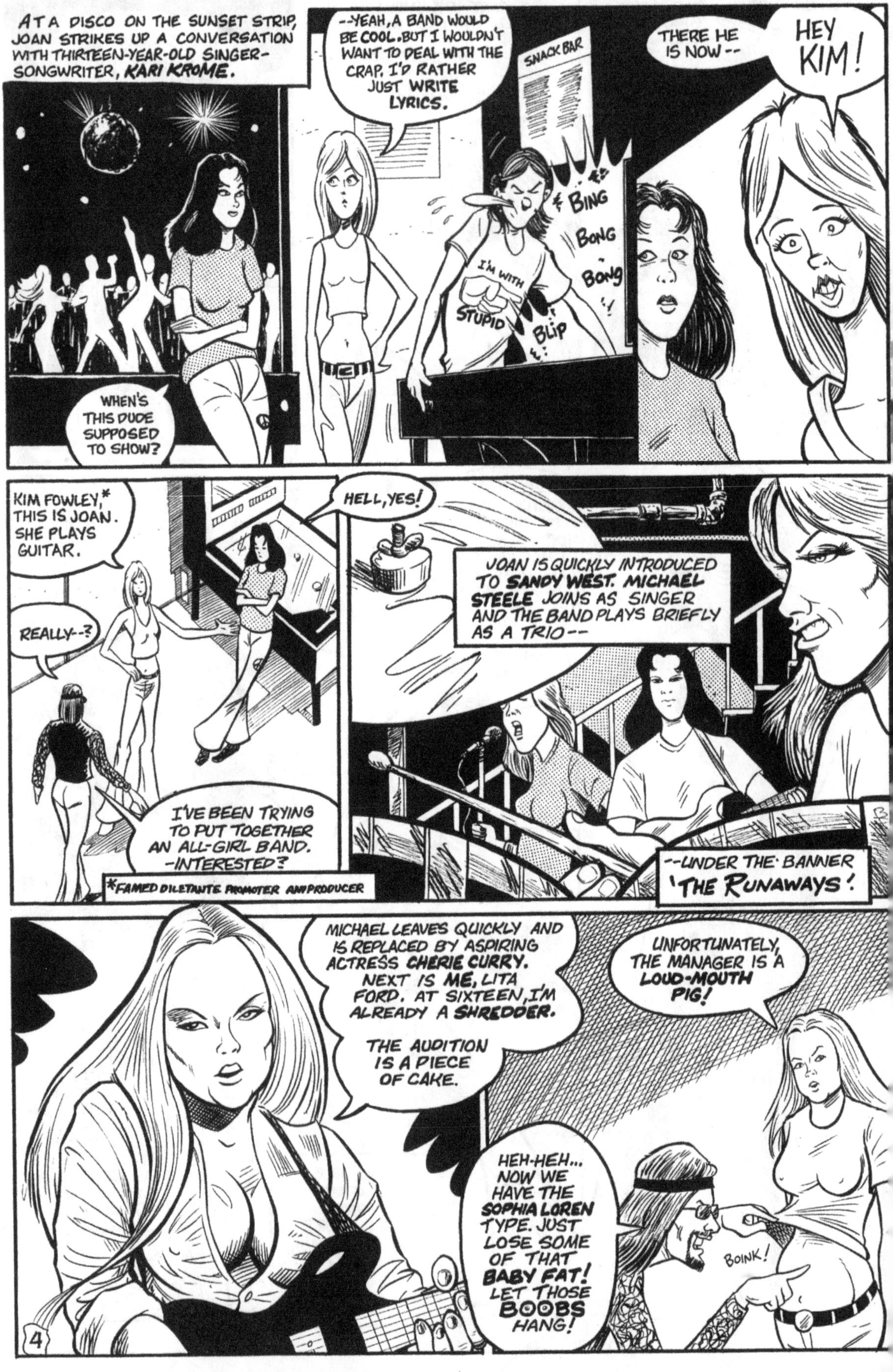
AT A DISCO ON THE SUNSET STRIP, JOAN STRIKES UP A CONVERSATION WITH THIRTEEN-YEAR-OLD SINGER-SONGWRITER, KARI KROME.
WHEN'S THIS DUDE SUPPOSED TO SHOW?
--YEAH, A BAND WOULD BE COOL. BUT I WOULDN'T WANT TO DEAL WITH THE CRAP. I'D RATHER JUST WRITE LYRICS.
SNACK BAR
I'M WITH STUPID
BING
BONG
BONG
BLIP
THERE HE IS NOW --
HEY KIM!
KIM FOWLEY,* THIS IS JOAN. SHE PLAYS GUITAR.
HELL, YES!
REALLY--?
I'VE BEEN TRYING TO PUT TOGETHER AN ALL-GIRL BAND. -INTERESTED?
*FAMED DILETANTE PROMOTER AND PRODUCER
JOAN IS QUICKLY INTRODUCED TO SANDY WEST. MICHAEL STEELE JOINS AS SINGER AND THE BAND PLAYS BRIEFLY AS A TRIO--
--UNDER THE BANNER 'THE RUNAWAYS'.
MICHAEL LEAVES QUICKLY AND IS REPLACED BY ASPIRING ACTRESS CHERIE CURRY. NEXT IS ME, LITA FORD. AT SIXTEEN, I'M ALREADY A SHREDDER.
THE AUDITION IS A PIECE OF CAKE.
UNFORTUNATELY, THE MANAGER IS A LOUD-MOUTH PIG!
HEH-HEH... NOW WE HAVE THE SOPHIA LOREN TYPE. JUST LOSE SOME OF THAT BABY FAT! LET THOSE BOOBS HANG!
BOINK!
4

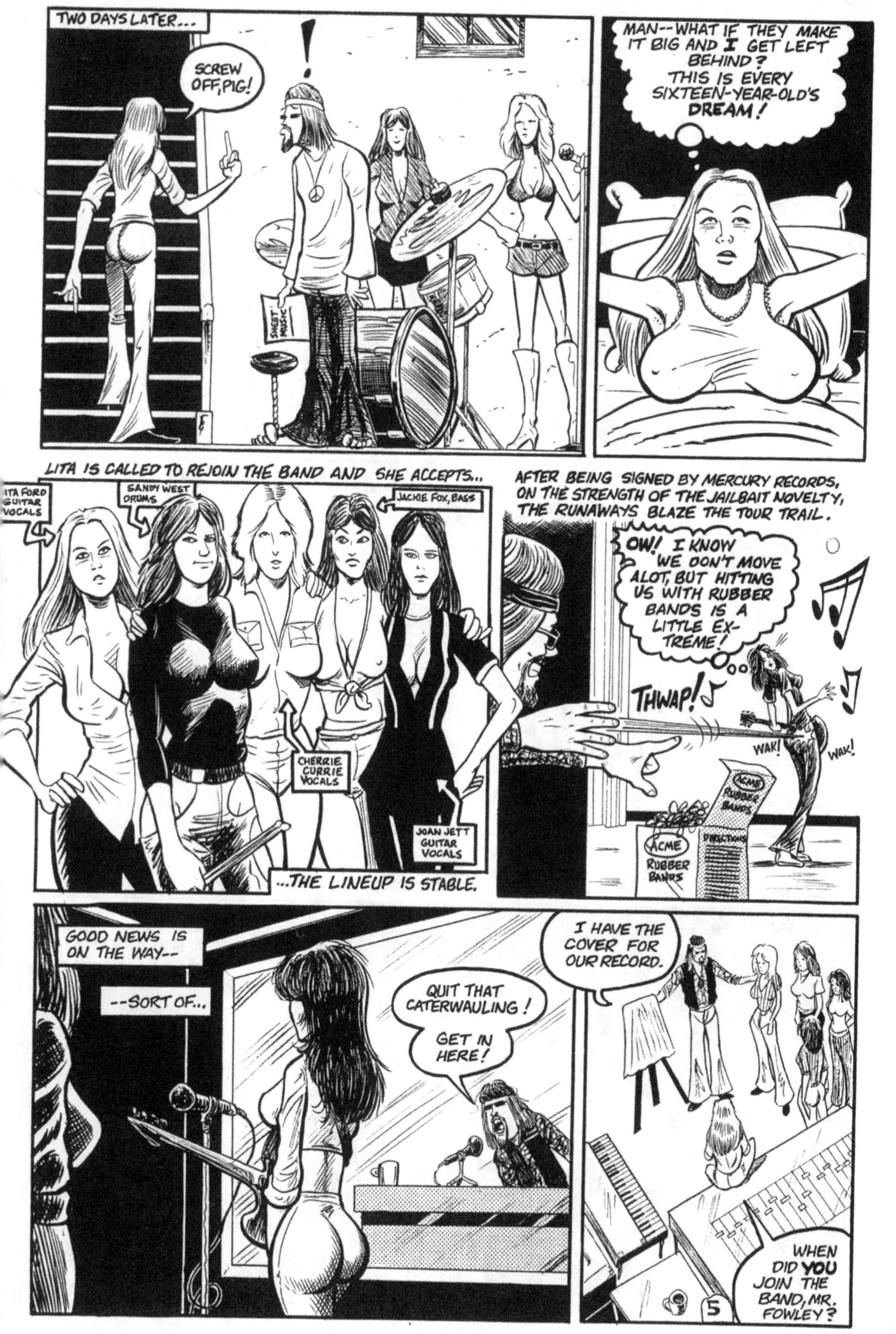
TWO DAYS LATER...
SCREW OFF, PIG!
!
SHEET MUSIC
MAN--WHAT IF THEY MAKE IT BIG AND I GET LEFT BEHIND? THIS IS EVERY SIXTEEN-YEAR-OLD'S DREAM!
LITA IS CALLED TO REJOIN THE BAND AND SHE ACCEPTS...
ITA FORD GUITAR VOCALS
SANDY WEST DRUMS
JACKIE FOX, BASS
CHERRIE CURRIE VOCALS
JOAN JETT GUITAR VOCALS
...THE LINEUP IS STABLE.
AFTER BEING SIGNED BY MERCURY RECORDS, ON THE STRENGTH OF THE JAILBAIT NOVELTY, THE RUNAWAYS BLAZE THE TOUR TRAIL.
OW! I KNOW WE DON'T MOVE ALOT, BUT HITTING US WITH RUBBER BANDS IS A LITTLE EX-TREME!
THWAP!
WAK!
WAK!
ACME RUBBER BANDS
ACME RUBBER BANDS
DIRECTIONS
GOOD NEWS IS ON THE WAY--
--SORT OF...
QUIT THAT CATERWAULING!
GET IN HERE!
I HAVE THE COVER FOR OUR RECORD.
WHEN DID YOU JOIN THE BAND, MR. FOWLEY?

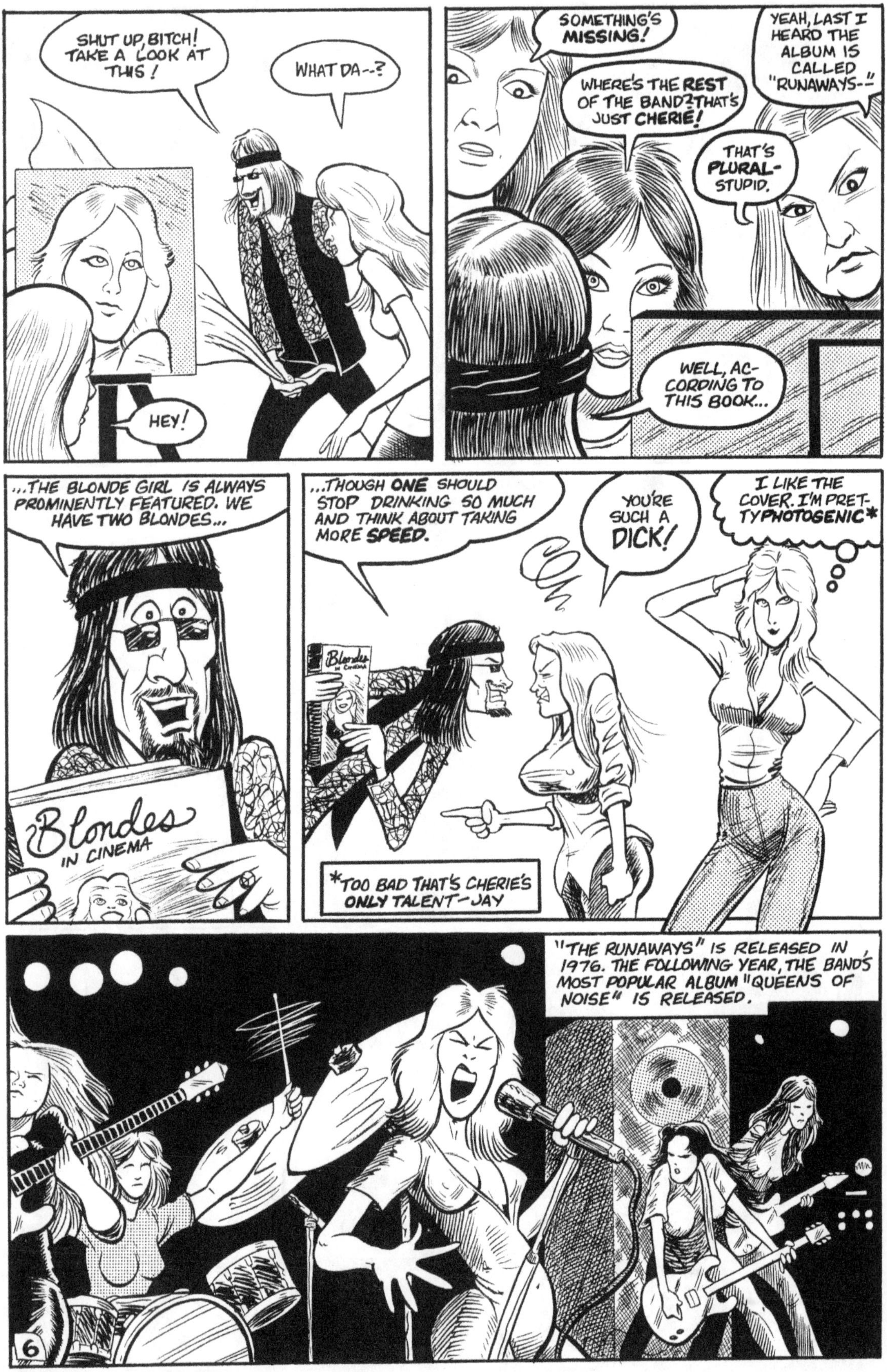
SHUT UP, BITCH! TAKE A LOOK AT THIS!
WHAT DA--?
HEY!
SOMETHING'S **MISSING**!
WHERE'S THE **REST** OF THE BAND? THAT'S JUST **CHERIÉ**!
YEAH, LAST I HEARD THE ALBUM IS CALLED "RUNAWAYS--"
THAT'S **PLURAL**- STUPID.
WELL, ACCORDING TO THIS BOOK...
...THE BLONDE GIRL IS ALWAYS PROMINENTLY FEATURED. WE HAVE TWO BLONDES...
Blondes IN CINEMA
...THOUGH **ONE** SHOULD STOP DRINKING SO MUCH AND THINK ABOUT TAKING MORE **SPEED**.
YOU'RE SUCH A DICK!
I LIKE THE COVER. I'M PRETTY **PHOTOGENIC***
*TOO BAD THAT'S CHERIE'S **ONLY TALENT** -JAY
"THE RUNAWAYS" IS RELEASED IN 1976. THE FOLLOWING YEAR, THE BAND'S MOST **POPULAR** ALBUM "QUEENS OF NOISE" IS RELEASED.

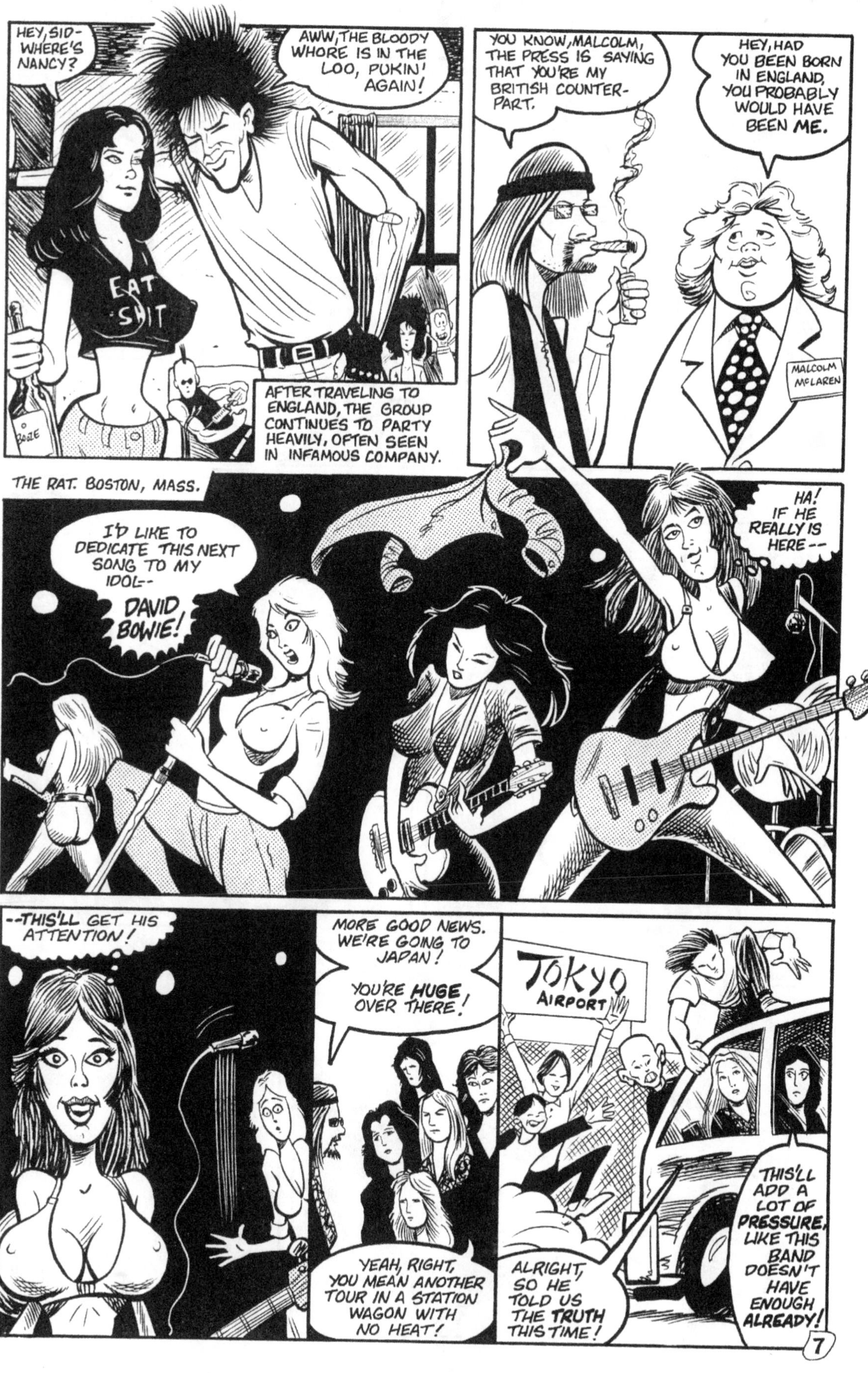

HEY, SID- WHERE'S NANCY?
AWW, THE BLOODY WHORE IS IN THE LOO, PUKIN' AGAIN!
EAT SHIT
BOOZE
AFTER TRAVELING TO ENGLAND, THE GROUP CONTINUES TO PARTY HEAVILY, OFTEN SEEN IN INFAMOUS COMPANY.
YOU KNOW, MALCOLM, THE PRESS IS SAYING THAT YOU'RE MY BRITISH COUNTER-PART.
HEY, HAD YOU BEEN BORN IN ENGLAND, YOU PROBABLY WOULD HAVE BEEN **ME.**
MALCOLM McLAREN
THE RAT. BOSTON, MASS.
I'D LIKE TO DEDICATE THIS NEXT SONG TO MY IDOL--
DAVID BOWIE!
HA! IF HE REALLY IS HERE--
--THIS'LL GET HIS ATTENTION!
MORE GOOD NEWS. WE'RE GOING TO JAPAN!
YOU'RE **HUGE** OVER THERE!
YEAH, RIGHT, YOU MEAN ANOTHER TOUR IN A STATION WAGON WITH NO HEAT!
TOKYO AIRPORT
ALRIGHT, SO HE TOLD US THE **TRUTH** THIS TIME!
THIS'LL ADD A LOT OF **PRESSURE**, LIKE THIS BAND DOESN'T HAVE ENOUGH **ALREADY**!

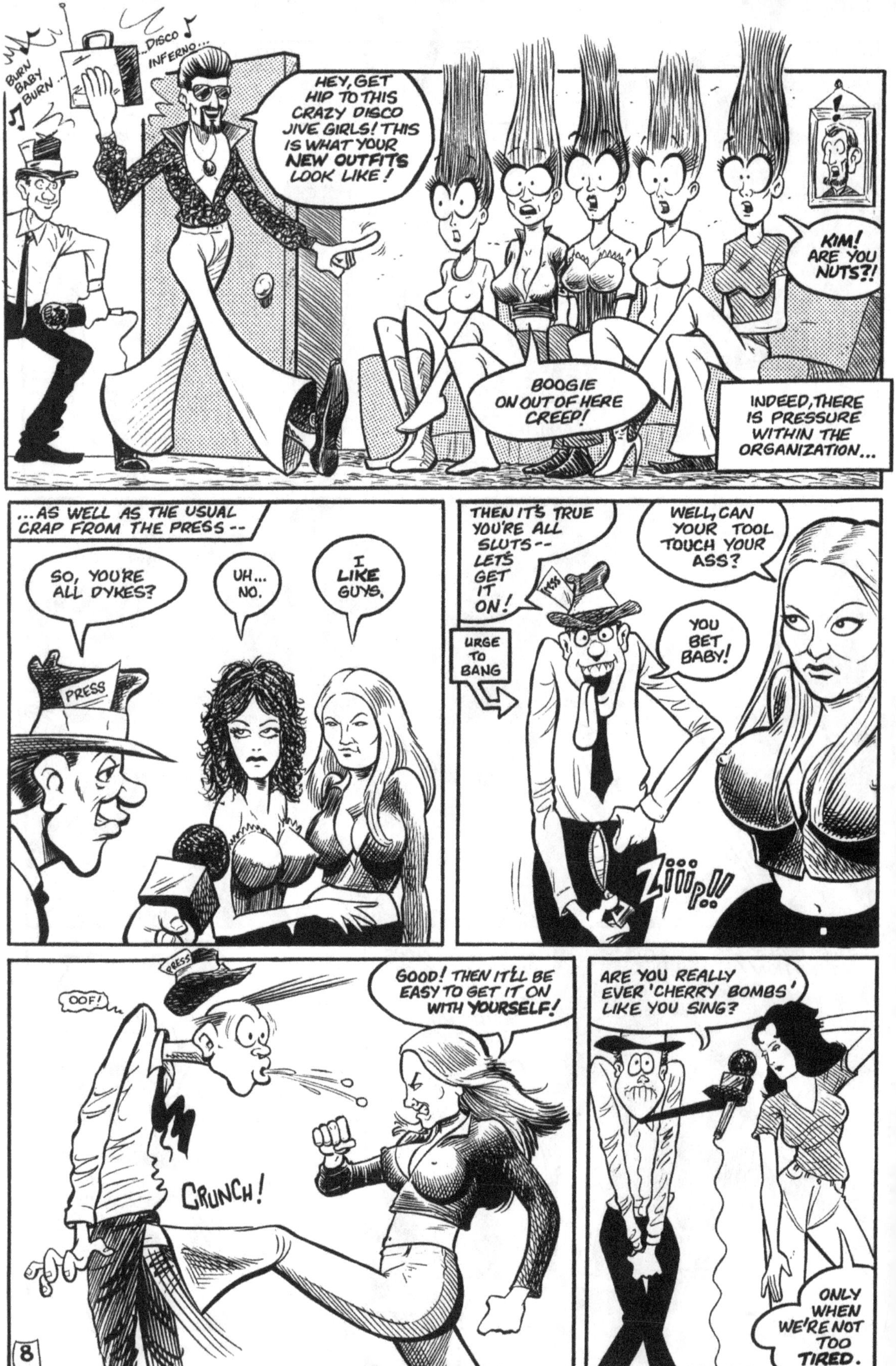
BURN BABY BURN...
...DISCO INFERNO...
HEY, GET HIP TO THIS CRAZY DISCO JIVE GIRLS! THIS IS WHAT YOUR NEW OUTFITS LOOK LIKE!
KIM! ARE YOU NUTS?!
BOOGIE ON OUT OF HERE CREEP!
INDEED, THERE IS PRESSURE WITHIN THE ORGANIZATION...
...AS WELL AS THE USUAL CRAP FROM THE PRESS --
SO, YOU'RE ALL DYKES?
UH... NO.
I LIKE GUYS.
PRESS
THEN IT'S TRUE YOU'RE ALL SLUTS -- LET'S GET IT ON!
WELL, CAN YOUR TOOL TOUCH YOUR ASS?
YOU BET BABY!
URGE TO BANG
ZIIIP!!
OOF!
GOOD! THEN IT'LL BE EASY TO GET IT ON WITH YOURSELF!
CRUNCH!
ARE YOU REALLY EVER 'CHERRY BOMBS' LIKE YOU SING?
ONLY WHEN WE'RE NOT TOO TIRED.

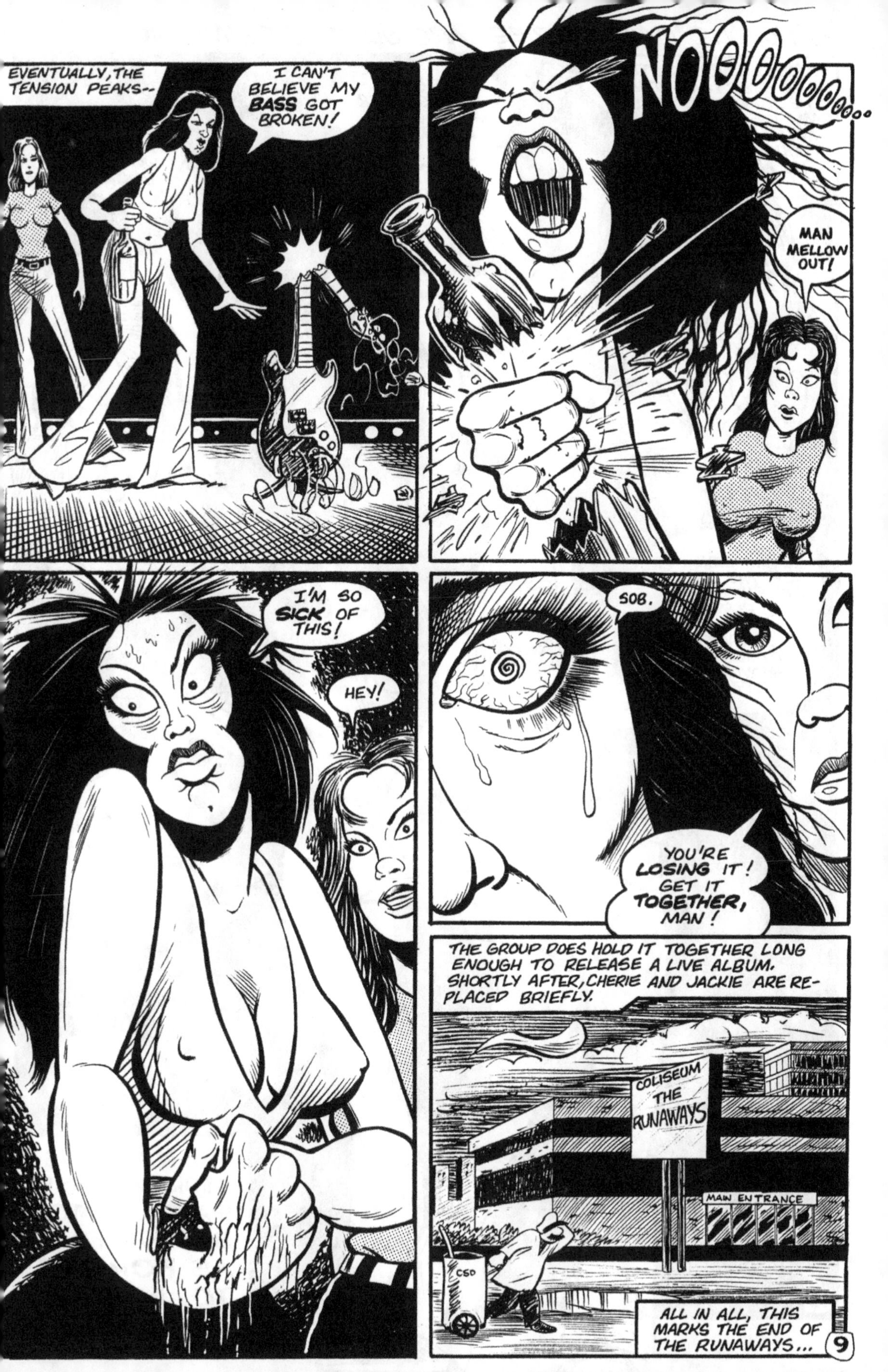

EVENTUALLY, THE TENSION PEAKS--
I CAN'T BELIEVE MY BASS GOT BROKEN!
NOOOOOOOooo
MAN MELLOW OUT!
I'M SO SICK OF THIS!
HEY!
SOB.
YOU'RE LOSING IT! GET IT TOGETHER, MAN!
THE GROUP DOES HOLD IT TOGETHER LONG ENOUGH TO RELEASE A LIVE ALBUM. SHORTLY AFTER, CHERIE AND JACKIE ARE REPLACED BRIEFLY.
COLISEUM THE RUNAWAYS
MAIN ENTRANCE
CSD
ALL IN ALL, THIS MARKS THE END OF THE RUNAWAYS...
9

-AND OUR MAIN STORIES ARE JUST **BEGINNING**...

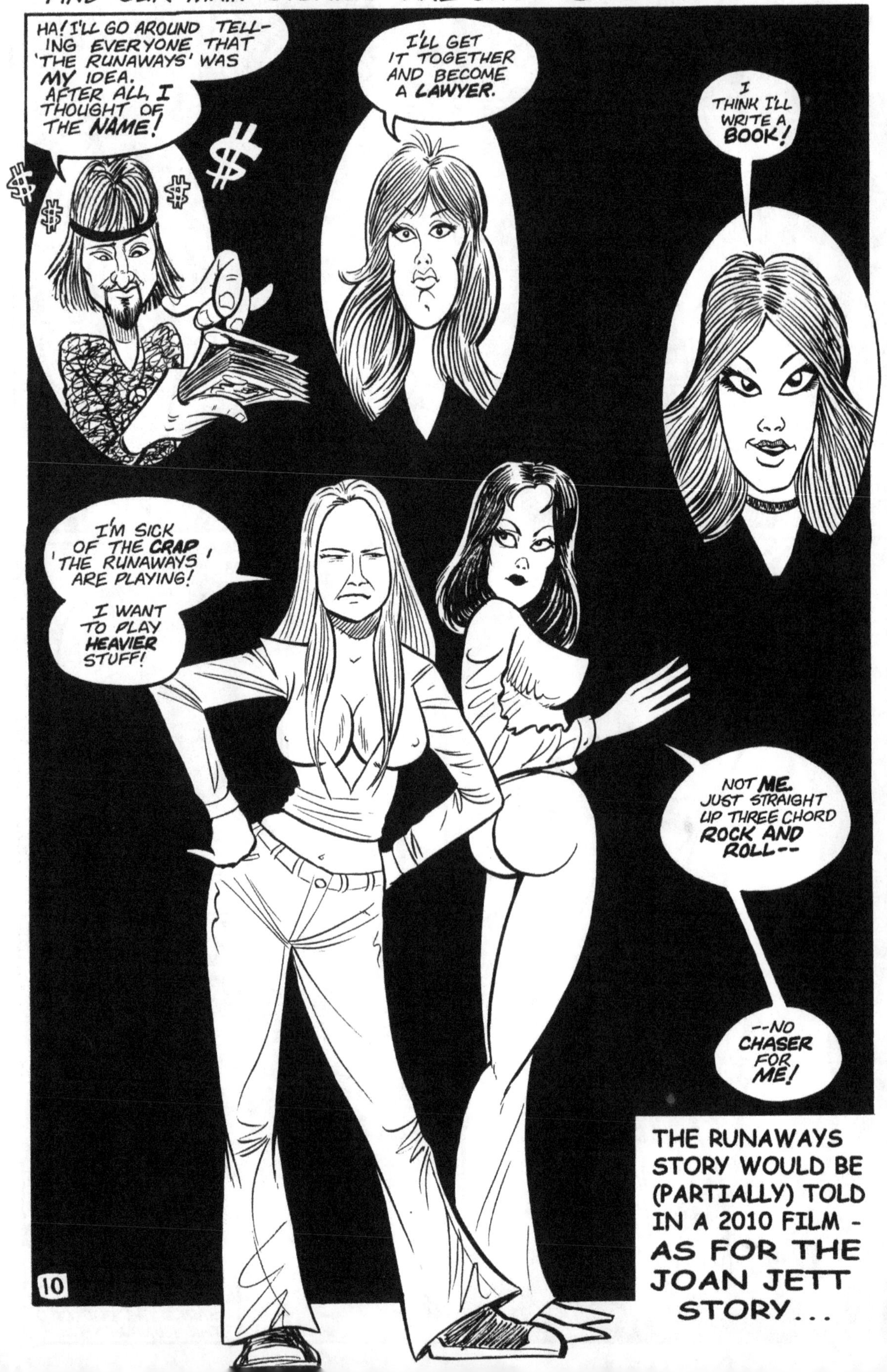

HA! I'LL GO AROUND TELLING EVERYONE THAT 'THE RUNAWAYS' WAS MY IDEA. AFTER ALL, I THOUGHT OF THE NAME!
$ $ $ $
I'LL GET IT TOGETHER AND BECOME A LAWYER.
I THINK I'LL WRITE A BOOK!
I'M SICK OF THE CRAP 'THE RUNAWAYS' ARE PLAYING!
I WANT TO PLAY HEAVIER STUFF!
NOT ME. JUST STRAIGHT UP THREE CHORD ROCK AND ROLL--
--NO CHASER FOR ME!
10
THE RUNAWAYS STORY WOULD BE (PARTIALLY) TOLD IN A 2010 FILM - AS FOR THE JOAN JETT STORY...

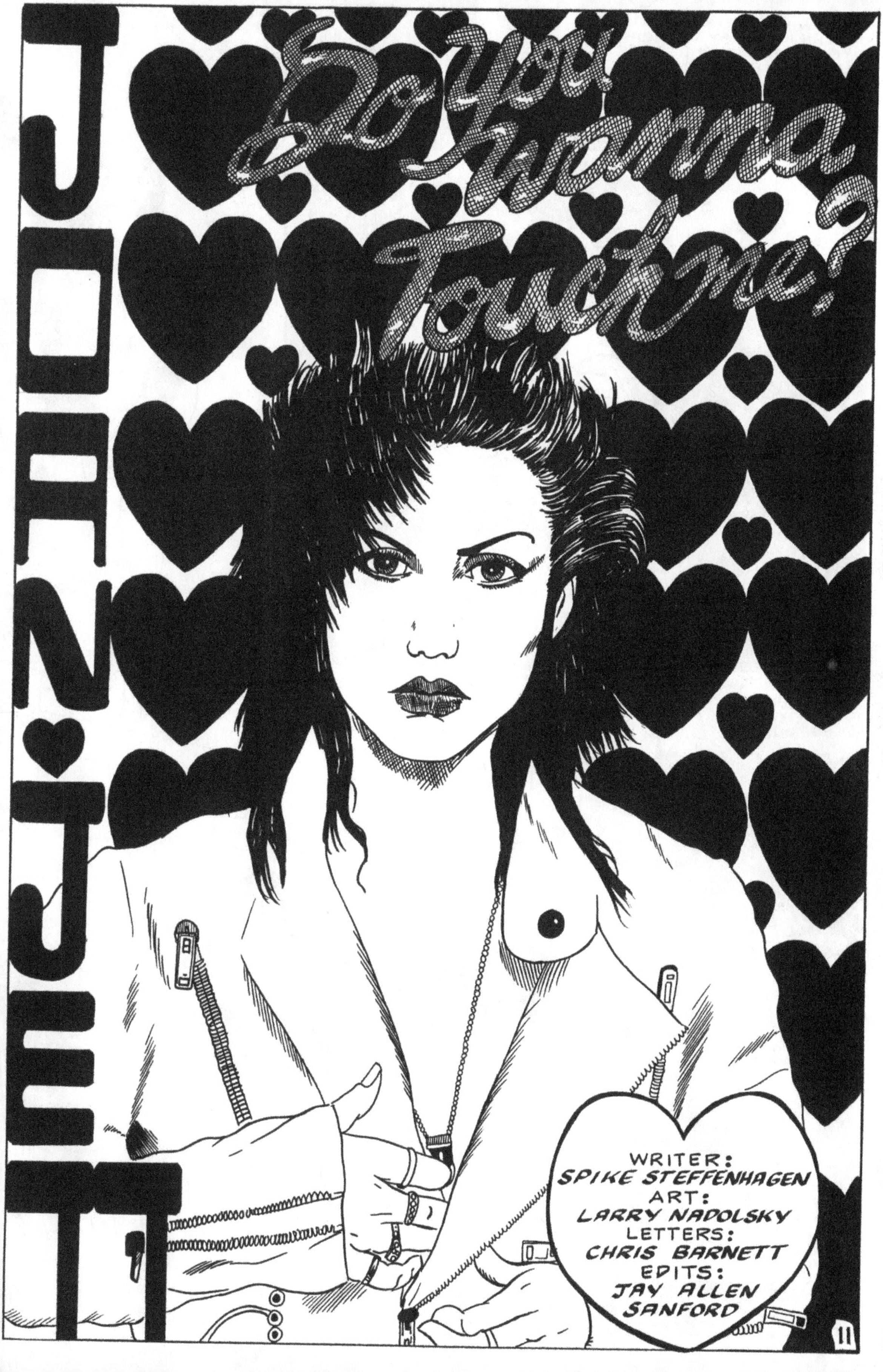
JOAN JETT
Do You Wanna Touch me?
WRITER: SPIKE STEFFENHAGEN
ART: LARRY NADOLSKY
LETTERS: CHRIS BARNETT
EDITS: JAY ALLEN SANFORD
11

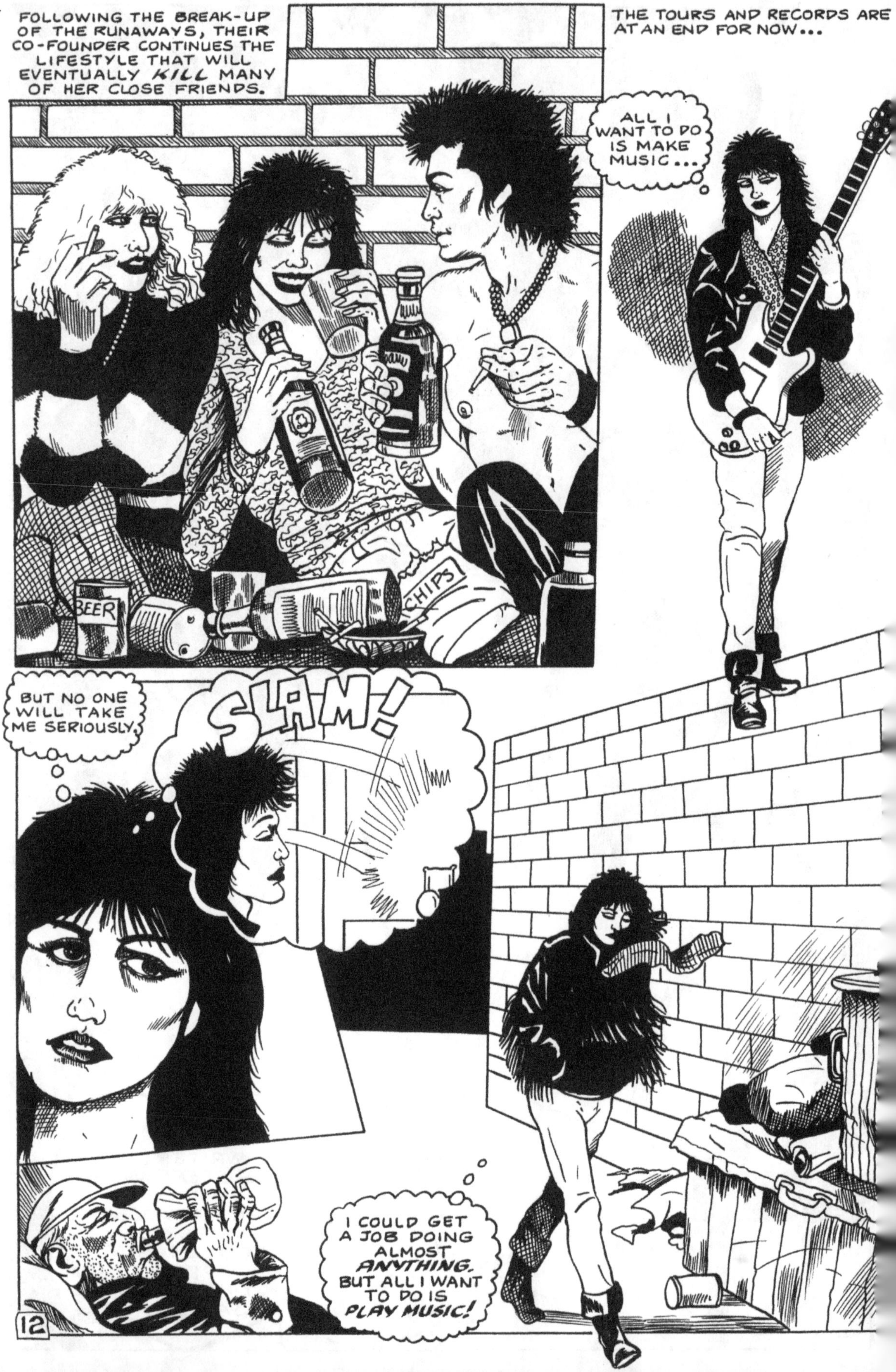

FOLLOWING THE BREAK-UP OF THE RUNAWAYS, THEIR CO-FOUNDER CONTINUES THE LIFESTYLE THAT WILL EVENTUALLY KILL MANY OF HER CLOSE FRIENDS.
BEER
CHIPS
THE TOURS AND RECORDS ARE AT AN END FOR NOW...
ALL I WANT TO DO IS MAKE MUSIC...
BUT NO ONE WILL TAKE ME SERIOUSLY.
SLAM!
I COULD GET A JOB DOING ALMOST ANYTHING, BUT ALL I WANT TO DO IS PLAY MUSIC!

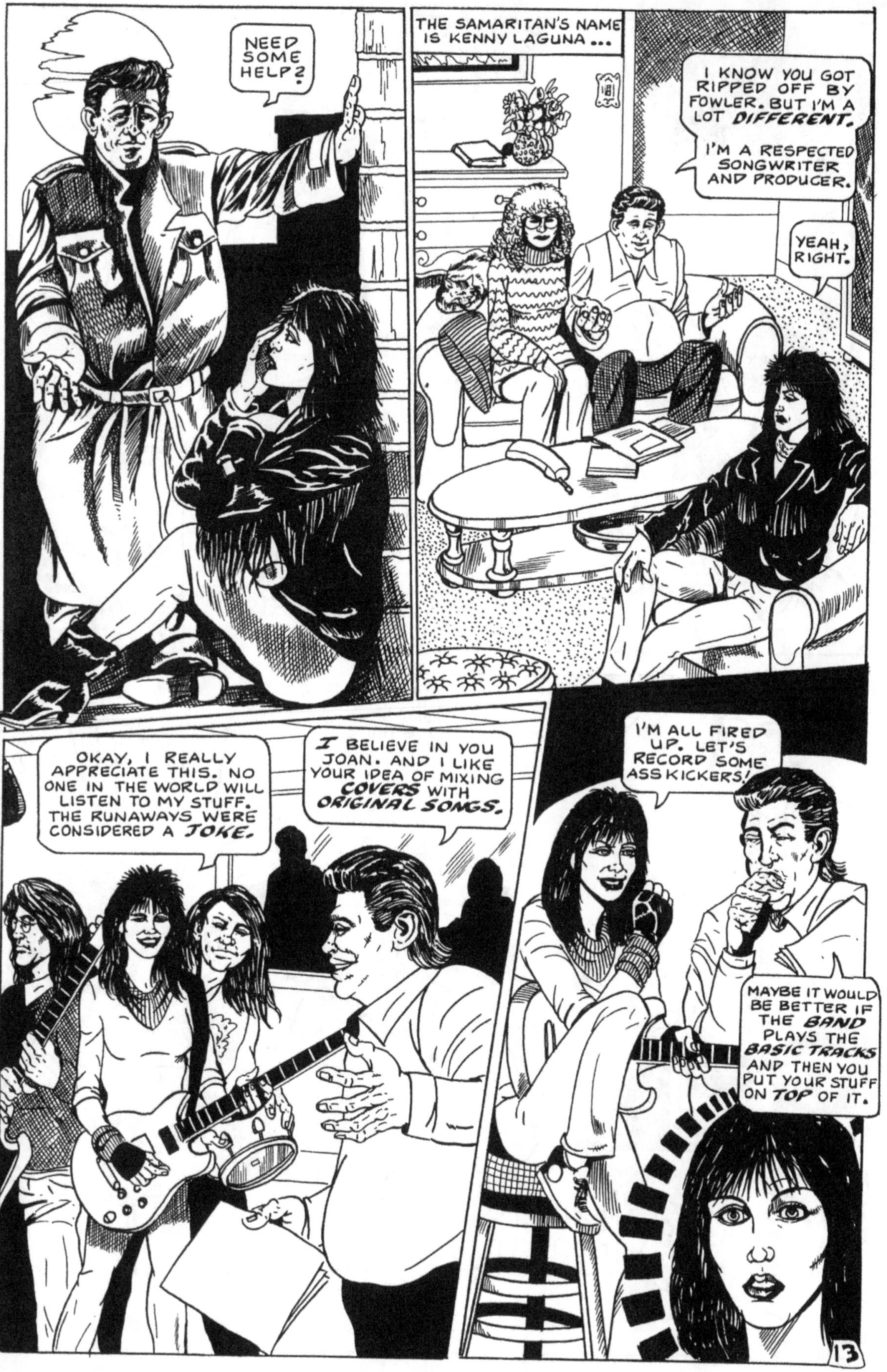
NEED SOME HELP?
THE SAMARITAN'S NAME IS KENNY LAGUNA...
I KNOW YOU GOT RIPPED OFF BY FOWLER. BUT I'M A LOT DIFFERENT.
I'M A RESPECTED SONGWRITER AND PRODUCER.
YEAH, RIGHT.
OKAY, I REALLY APPRECIATE THIS. NO ONE IN THE WORLD WILL LISTEN TO MY STUFF. THE RUNAWAYS WERE CONSIDERED A JOKE.
I BELIEVE IN YOU JOAN. AND I LIKE YOUR IDEA OF MIXING COVERS WITH ORIGINAL SONGS.
I'M ALL FIRED UP. LET'S RECORD SOME ASS KICKERS!
MAYBE IT WOULD BE BETTER IF THE BAND PLAYS THE BASIC TRACKS AND THEN YOU PUT YOUR STUFF ON TOP OF IT.

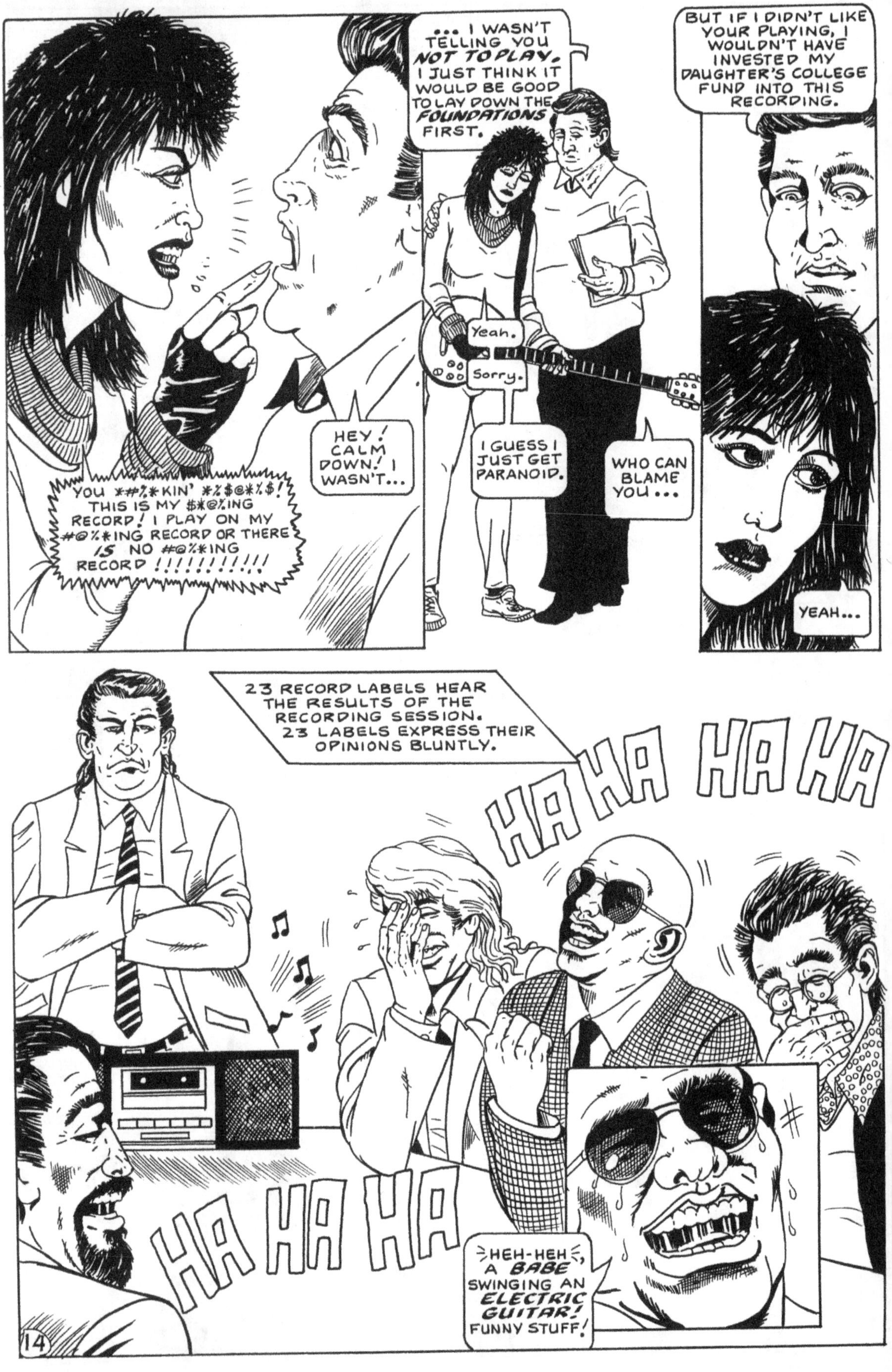
YOU *#%*KIN' *%$@*%$! THIS IS MY $*@%ING RECORD! I PLAY ON MY #@%*ING RECORD OR THERE IS NO #@%*ING RECORD!!!!!!!!!!!
HEY! CALM DOWN! I WASN'T...
... I WASN'T TELLING YOU NOT TO PLAY. I JUST THINK IT WOULD BE GOOD TO LAY DOWN THE FOUNDATIONS FIRST.
Yeah.
Sorry.
I GUESS I JUST GET PARANOID.
WHO CAN BLAME YOU...
BUT IF I DIDN'T LIKE YOUR PLAYING, I WOULDN'T HAVE INVESTED MY DAUGHTER'S COLLEGE FUND INTO THIS RECORDING.
YEAH...
23 RECORD LABELS HEAR THE RESULTS OF THE RECORDING SESSION. 23 LABELS EXPRESS THEIR OPINIONS BLUNTLY.
HA HA HA HA HA
HA HA HA HA
HEH-HEH, A BABE SWINGING AN ELECTRIC GUITAR! FUNNY STUFF!

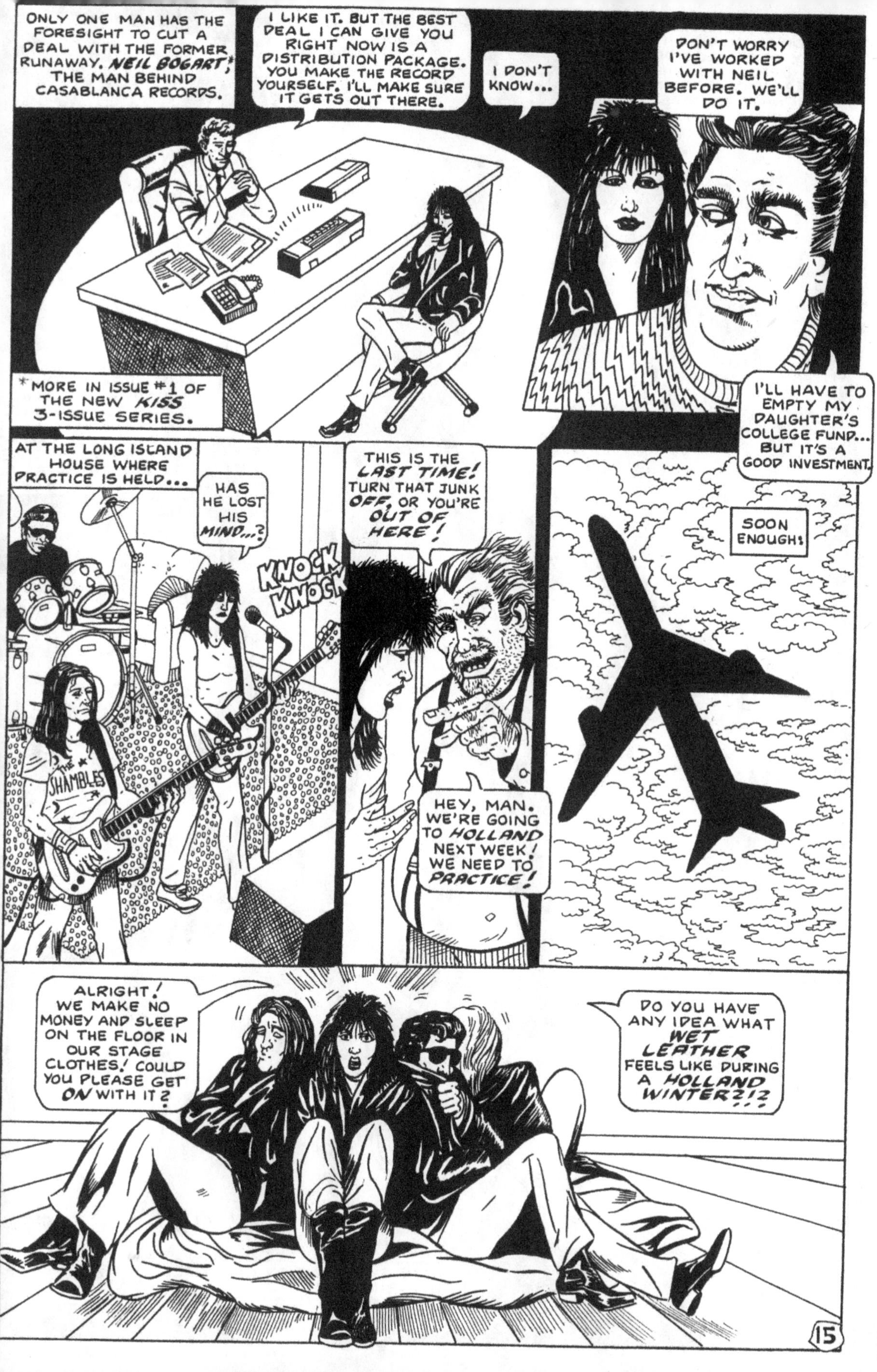

ONLY ONE MAN HAS THE FORESIGHT TO CUT A DEAL WITH THE FORMER RUNAWAY. NEIL BOGART*, THE MAN BEHIND CASABLANCA RECORDS.
I LIKE IT. BUT THE BEST DEAL I CAN GIVE YOU RIGHT NOW IS A DISTRIBUTION PACKAGE. YOU MAKE THE RECORD YOURSELF. I'LL MAKE SURE IT GETS OUT THERE.
I DON'T KNOW...
DON'T WORRY I'VE WORKED WITH NEIL BEFORE. WE'LL DO IT.
*MORE IN ISSUE #1 OF THE NEW KISS 3-ISSUE SERIES.
I'LL HAVE TO EMPTY MY DAUGHTER'S COLLEGE FUND... BUT IT'S A GOOD INVESTMENT.
AT THE LONG ISLAND HOUSE WHERE PRACTICE IS HELD...
HAS HE LOST HIS MIND...?
KNOCK KNOCK
THIS IS THE LAST TIME! TURN THAT JUNK OFF, OR YOU'RE OUT OF HERE!
HEY, MAN. WE'RE GOING TO HOLLAND NEXT WEEK! WE NEED TO PRACTICE!
SOON ENOUGH:
ALRIGHT! WE MAKE NO MONEY AND SLEEP ON THE FLOOR IN OUR STAGE CLOTHES! COULD YOU PLEASE GET ON WITH IT?
DO YOU HAVE ANY IDEA WHAT WET LEATHER FEELS LIKE DURING A HOLLAND WINTER?!?
15

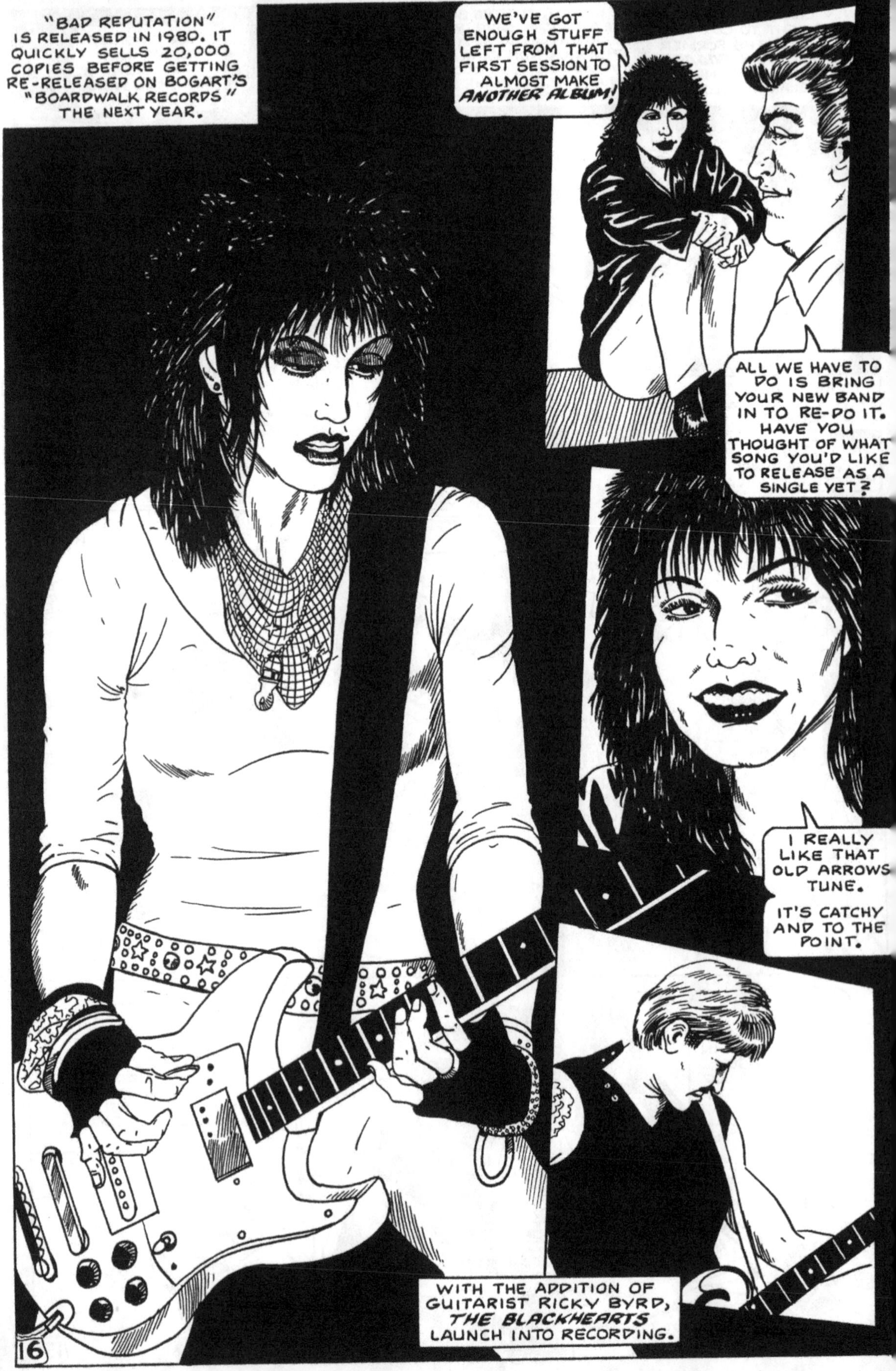
"BAD REPUTATION" IS RELEASED IN 1980. IT QUICKLY SELLS 20,000 COPIES BEFORE GETTING RE-RELEASED ON BOGART'S "BOARDWALK RECORDS" THE NEXT YEAR.
WE'VE GOT ENOUGH STUFF LEFT FROM THAT FIRST SESSION TO ALMOST MAKE ANOTHER ALBUM!
ALL WE HAVE TO DO IS BRING YOUR NEW BAND IN TO RE-DO IT. HAVE YOU THOUGHT OF WHAT SONG YOU'D LIKE TO RELEASE AS A SINGLE YET?
I REALLY LIKE THAT OLD ARROWS TUNE.
IT'S CATCHY AND TO THE POINT.
WITH THE ADDITION OF GUITARIST RICKY BYRD, THE BLACKHEARTS LAUNCH INTO RECORDING.

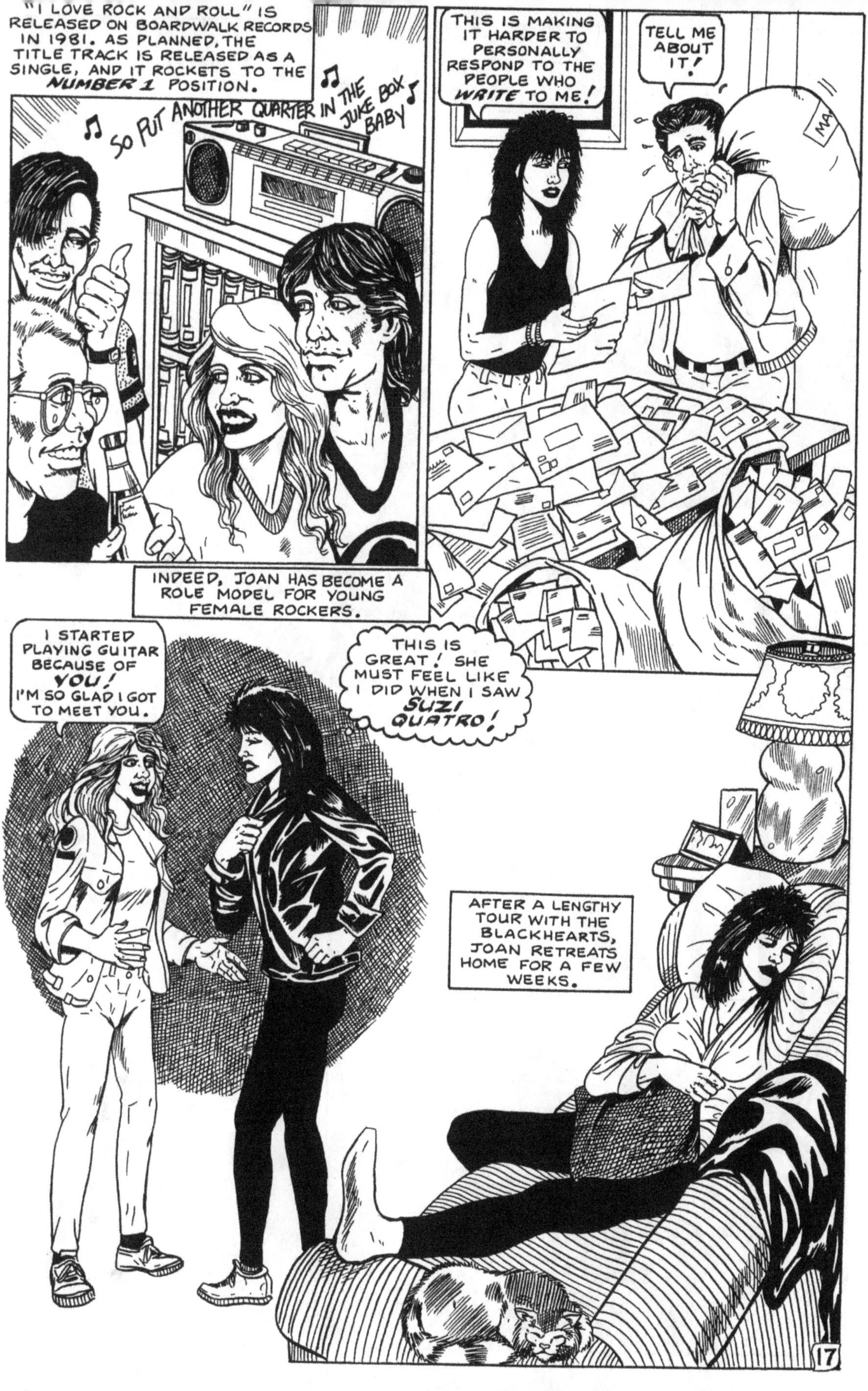
"I LOVE ROCK AND ROLL" IS RELEASED ON BOARDWALK RECORDS IN 1981. AS PLANNED, THE TITLE TRACK IS RELEASED AS A SINGLE, AND IT ROCKETS TO THE NUMBER 1 POSITION.
SO PUT ANOTHER QUARTER IN THE JUKE BOX BABY
INDEED, JOAN HAS BECOME A ROLE MODEL FOR YOUNG FEMALE ROCKERS.
THIS IS MAKING IT HARDER TO PERSONALLY RESPOND TO THE PEOPLE WHO WRITE TO ME!
TELL ME ABOUT IT!
I STARTED PLAYING GUITAR BECAUSE OF YOU! I'M SO GLAD I GOT TO MEET YOU.
THIS IS GREAT! SHE MUST FEEL LIKE I DID WHEN I SAW SUZI QUATRO!
AFTER A LENGTHY TOUR WITH THE BLACKHEARTS, JOAN RETREATS HOME FOR A FEW WEEKS.

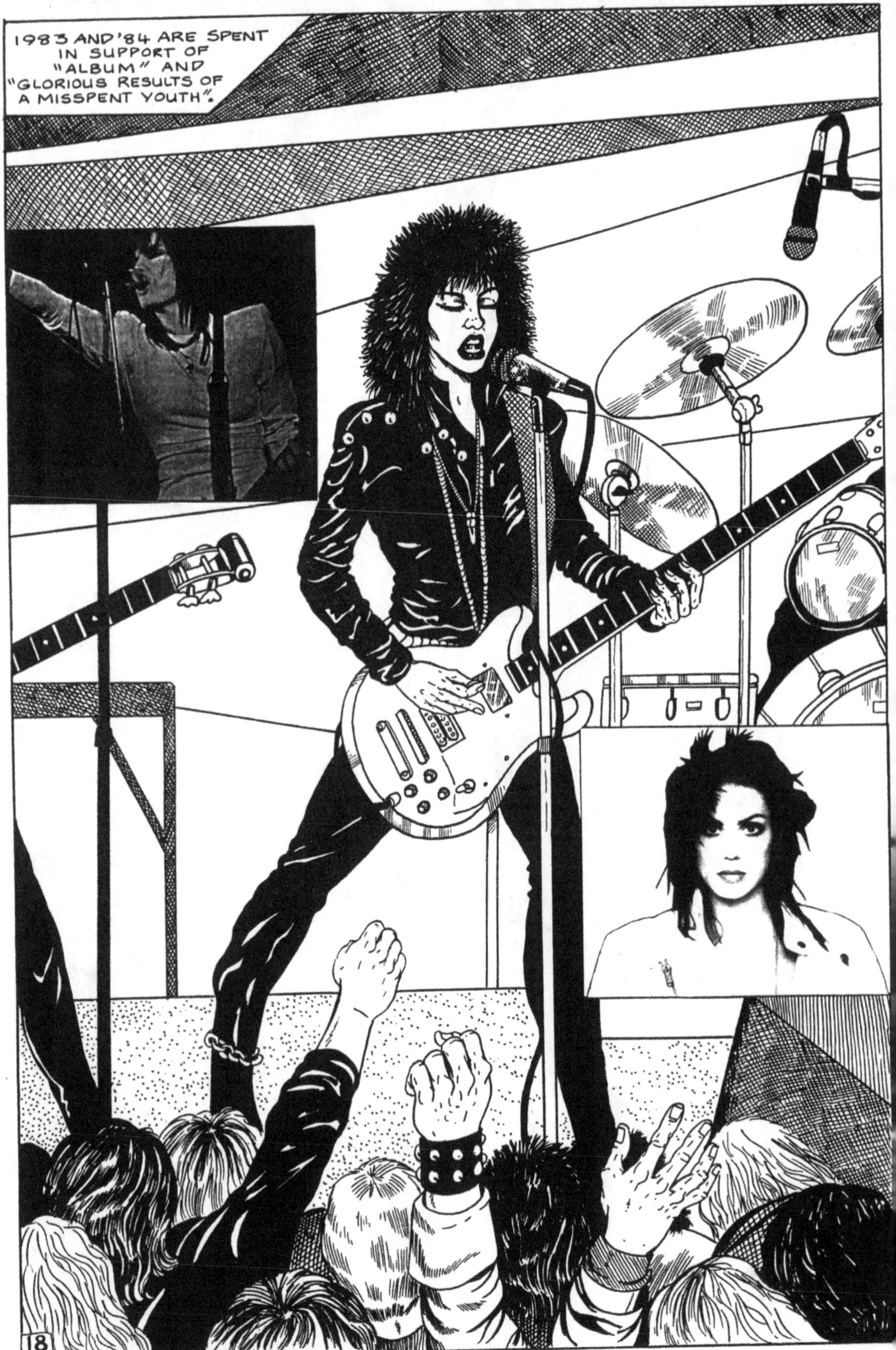
1983 AND '84 ARE SPENT IN SUPPORT OF "ALBUM" AND "GLORIOUS RESULTS OF A MISSPENT YOUTH".

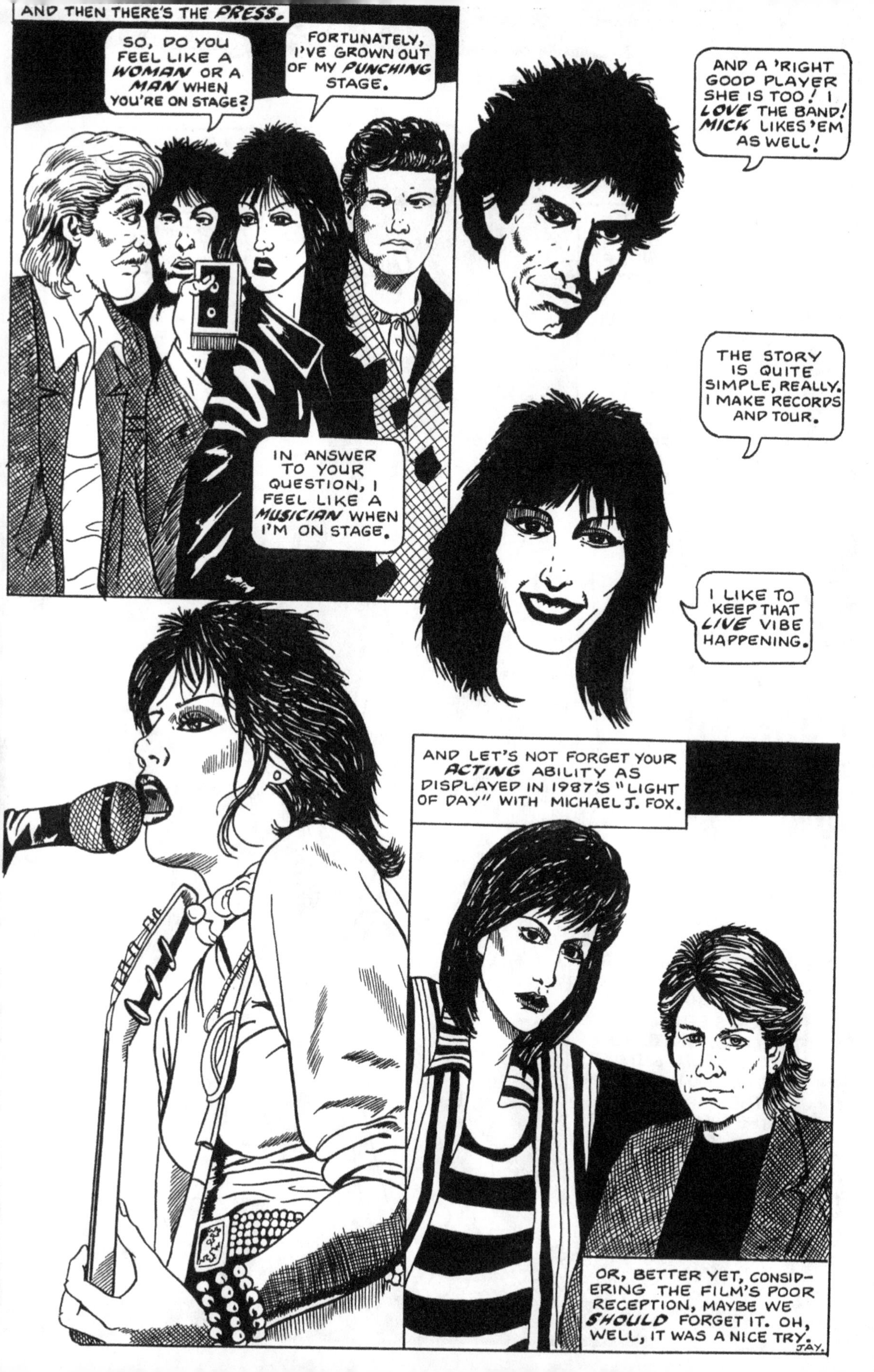
AND THEN THERE'S THE PRESS.
SO, DO YOU FEEL LIKE A WOMAN OR A MAN WHEN YOU'RE ON STAGE?
FORTUNATELY, I'VE GROWN OUT OF MY PUNCHING STAGE.
IN ANSWER TO YOUR QUESTION, I FEEL LIKE A MUSICIAN WHEN I'M ON STAGE.
AND A 'RIGHT GOOD PLAYER SHE IS TOO! I LOVE THE BAND! MICK LIKES 'EM AS WELL!
THE STORY IS QUITE SIMPLE, REALLY. I MAKE RECORDS AND TOUR.
I LIKE TO KEEP THAT LIVE VIBE HAPPENING.
AND LET'S NOT FORGET YOUR ACTING ABILITY AS DISPLAYED IN 1987'S "LIGHT OF DAY" WITH MICHAEL J. FOX.
OR, BETTER YET, CONSIDERING THE FILM'S POOR RECEPTION, MAYBE WE SHOULD FORGET IT. OH, WELL, IT WAS A NICE TRY.
JAY.

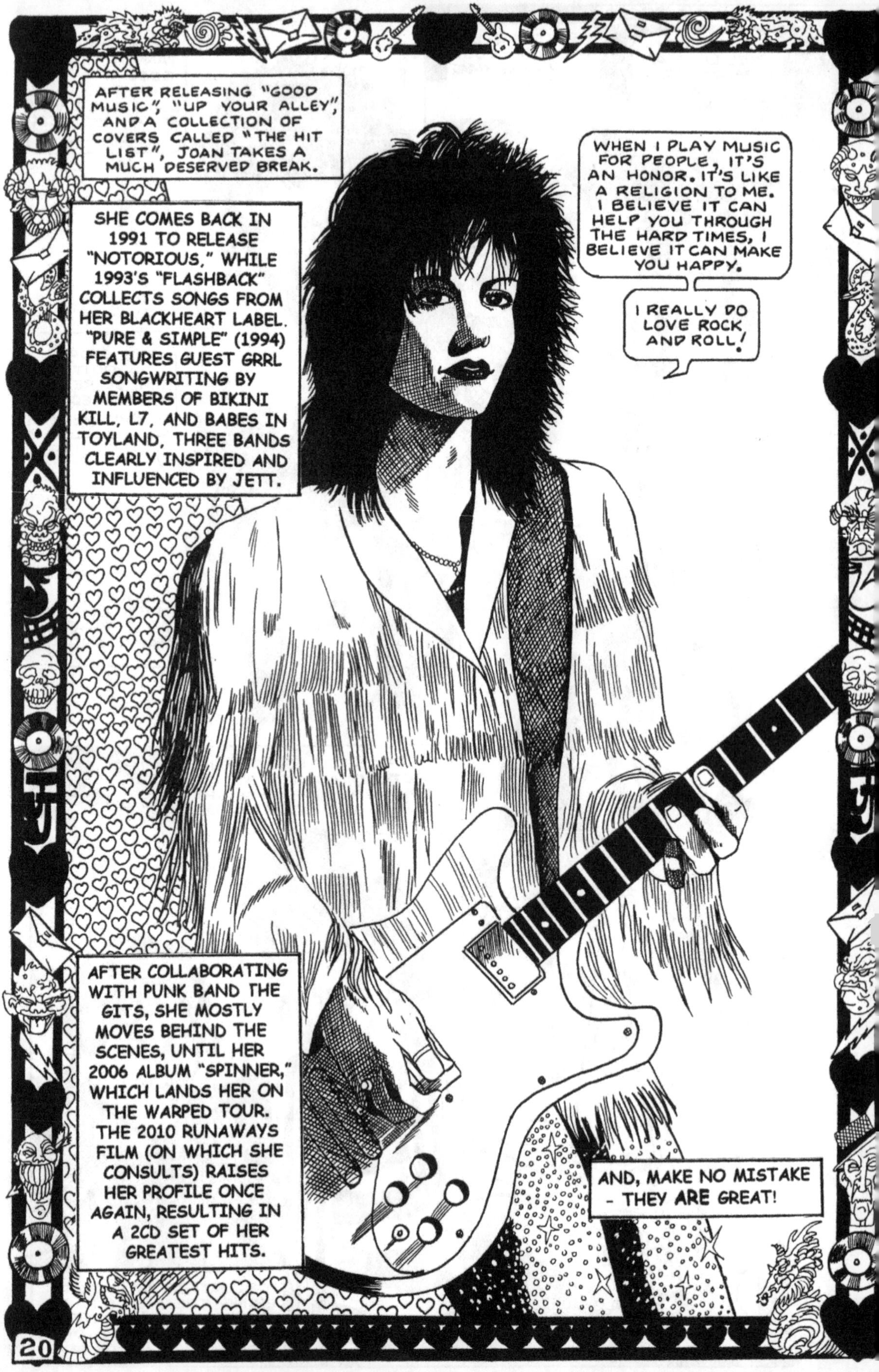
AFTER RELEASING "GOOD MUSIC", "UP YOUR ALLEY", AND A COLLECTION OF COVERS CALLED "THE HIT LIST", JOAN TAKES A MUCH DESERVED BREAK.
WHEN I PLAY MUSIC FOR PEOPLE, IT'S AN HONOR. IT'S LIKE A RELIGION TO ME. I BELIEVE IT CAN HELP YOU THROUGH THE HARD TIMES, I BELIEVE IT CAN MAKE YOU HAPPY.
I REALLY DO LOVE ROCK AND ROLL!
SHE COMES BACK IN 1991 TO RELEASE "NOTORIOUS," WHILE 1993'S "FLASHBACK" COLLECTS SONGS FROM HER BLACKHEART LABEL. "PURE & SIMPLE" (1994) FEATURES GUEST GRRL SONGWRITING BY MEMBERS OF BIKINI KILL, L7, AND BABES IN TOYLAND, THREE BANDS CLEARLY INSPIRED AND INFLUENCED BY JETT.
AFTER COLLABORATING WITH PUNK BAND THE GITS, SHE MOSTLY MOVES BEHIND THE SCENES, UNTIL HER 2006 ALBUM "SPINNER," WHICH LANDS HER ON THE WARPED TOUR. THE 2010 RUNAWAYS FILM (ON WHICH SHE CONSULTS) RAISES HER PROFILE ONCE AGAIN, RESULTING IN A 2CD SET OF HER GREATEST HITS.
AND, MAKE NO MISTAKE - THEY ARE GREAT!

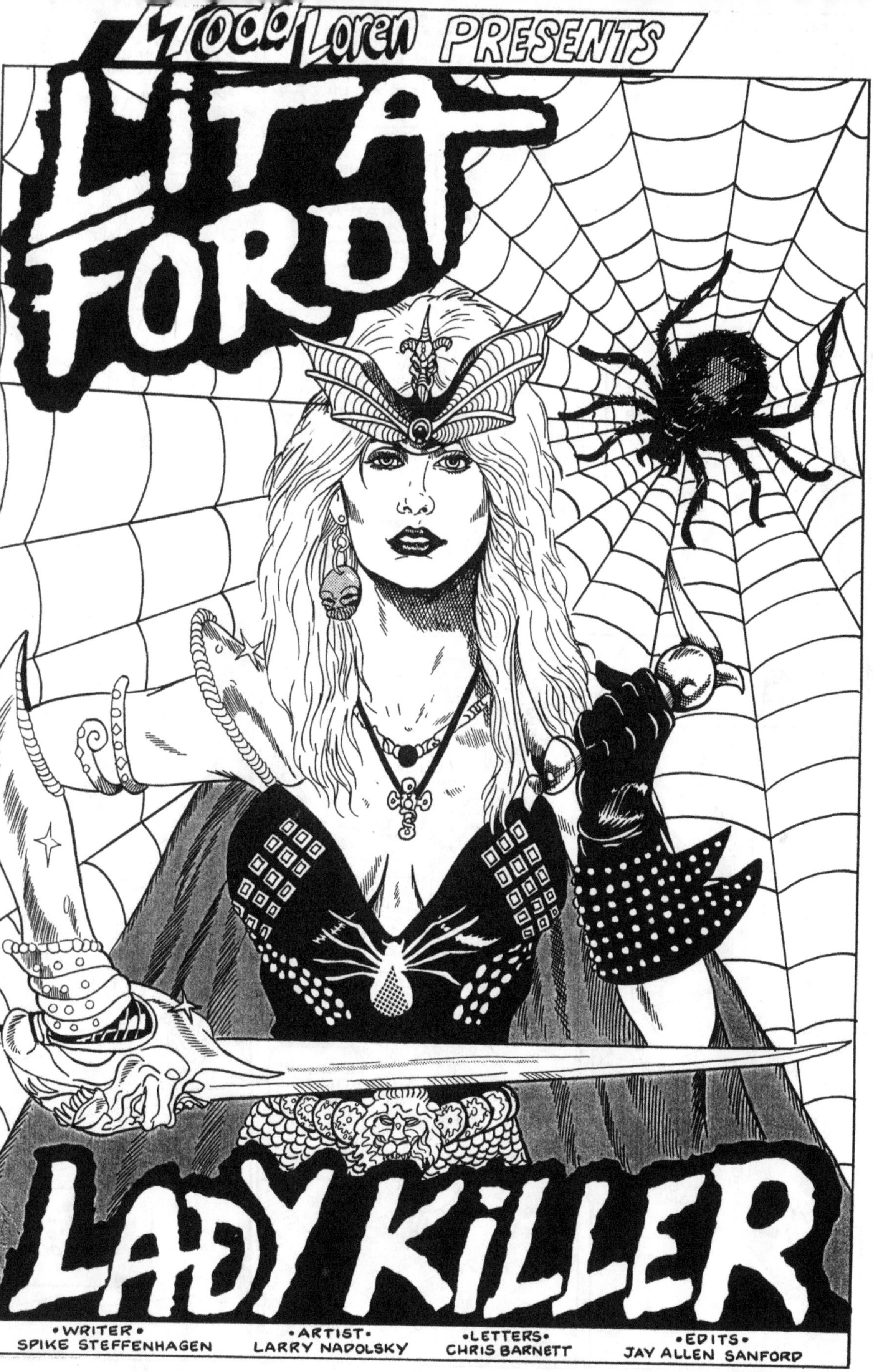
Todd Loren PRESENTS
LITA FORD
LADY KILLER

•WRITER• SPIKE STEFFENHAGEN
•ARTIST• LARRY NADOLSKY
•LETTERS• CHRIS BARNETT
•EDITS• JAY ALLEN SANFORD

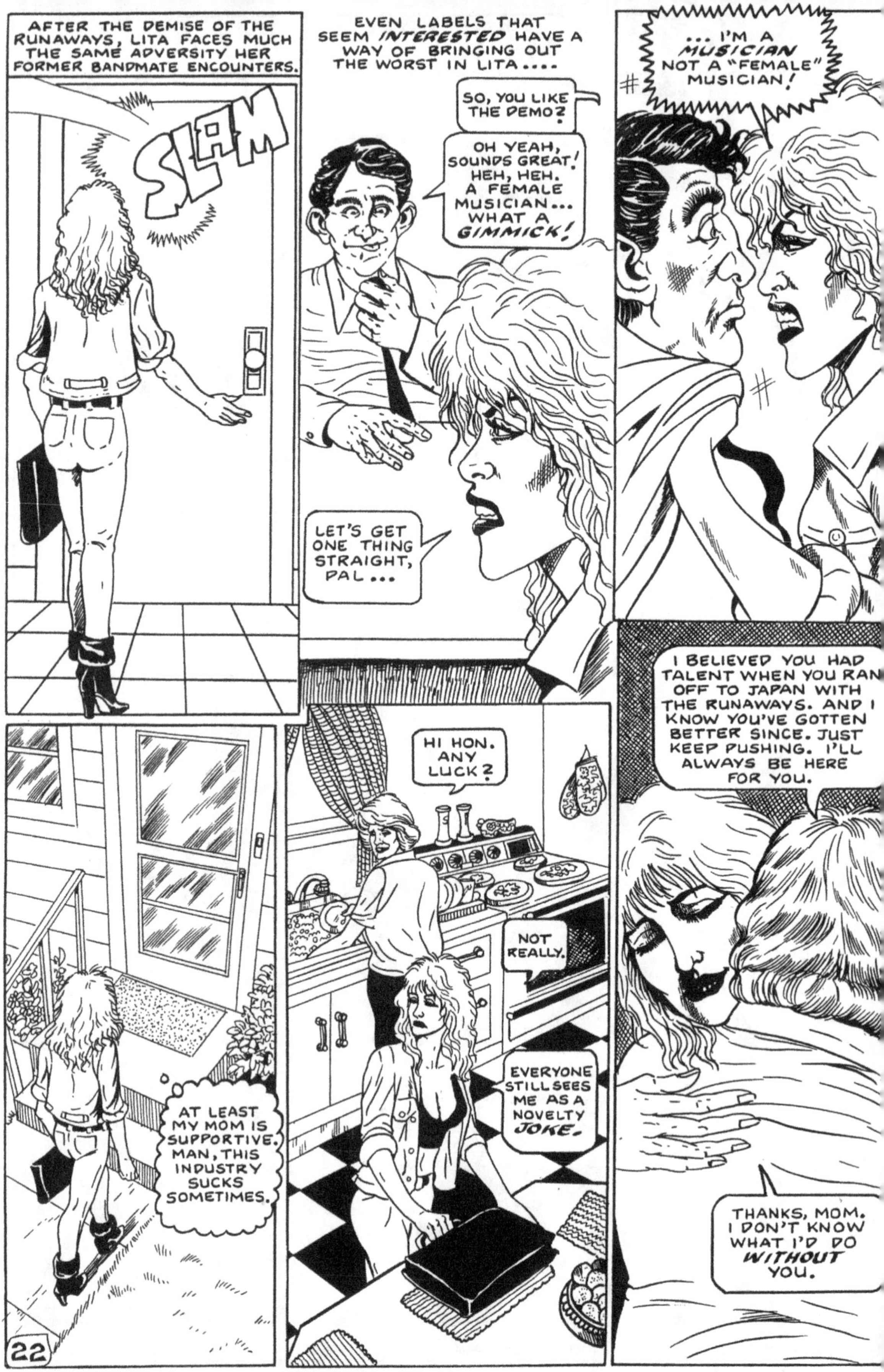
AFTER THE DEMISE OF THE RUNAWAYS, LITA FACES MUCH THE SAME ADVERSITY HER FORMER BANDMATE ENCOUNTERS.
SLAM
EVEN LABELS THAT SEEM *INTERESTED* HAVE A WAY OF BRINGING OUT THE WORST IN LITA....
SO, YOU LIKE THE DEMO?
OH YEAH, SOUNDS GREAT! HEH, HEH. A FEMALE MUSICIAN... WHAT A *GIMMICK!*
LET'S GET ONE THING STRAIGHT, PAL...
... I'M A *MUSICIAN* NOT A "FEMALE" MUSICIAN!
AT LEAST MY MOM IS SUPPORTIVE. MAN, THIS INDUSTRY SUCKS SOMETIMES.
HI HON. ANY LUCK?
NOT REALLY.
EVERYONE STILL SEES ME AS A NOVELTY *JOKE.*
I BELIEVED YOU HAD TALENT WHEN YOU RAN OFF TO JAPAN WITH THE RUNAWAYS. AND I KNOW YOU'VE GOTTEN BETTER SINCE. JUST KEEP PUSHING. I'LL ALWAYS BE HERE FOR YOU.
THANKS, MOM. I DON'T KNOW WHAT I'D DO *WITHOUT* YOU.

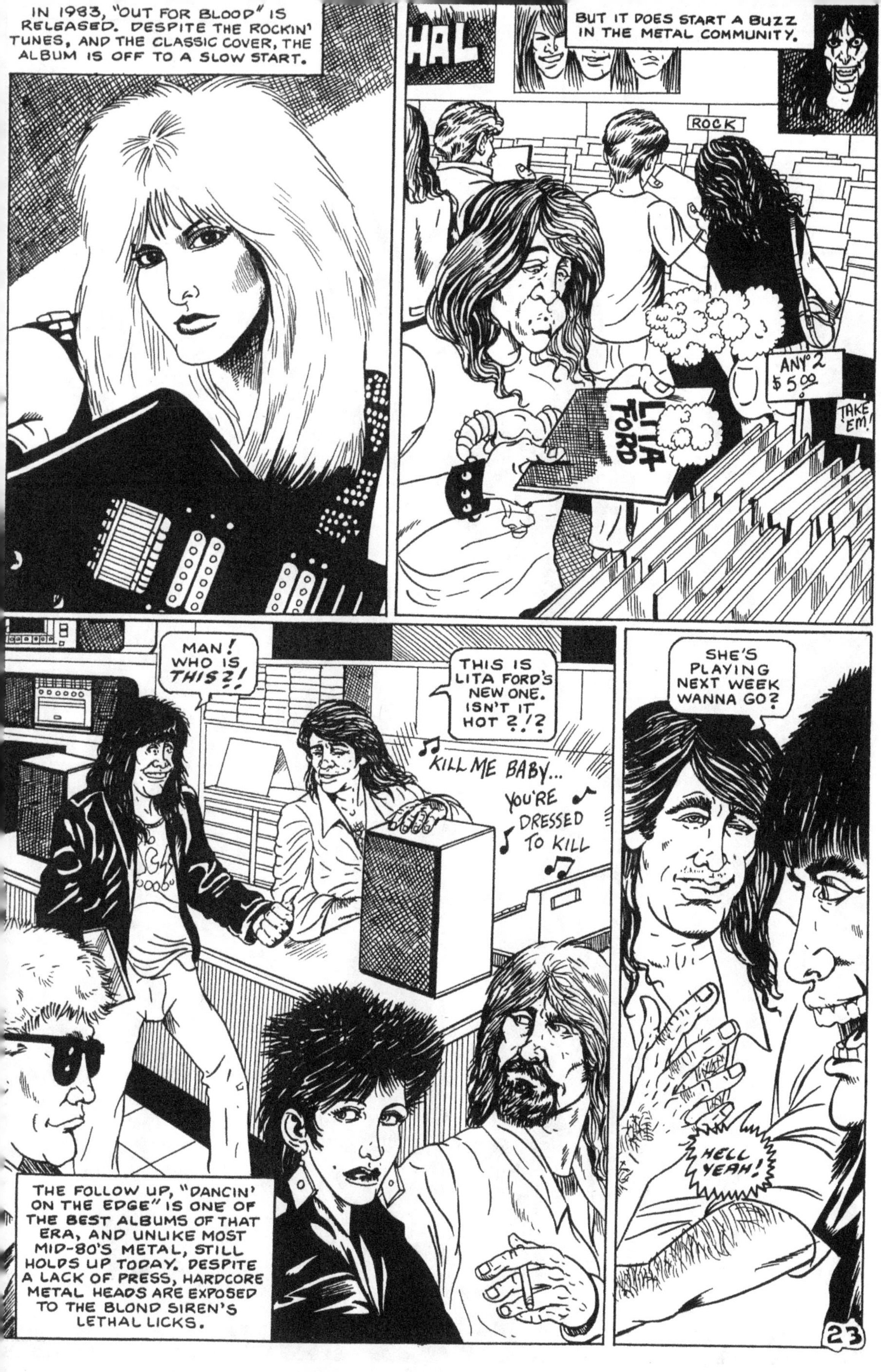

IN 1983, "OUT FOR BLOOD" IS RELEASED. DESPITE THE ROCKIN' TUNES, AND THE CLASSIC COVER, THE ALBUM IS OFF TO A SLOW START.
BUT IT DOES START A BUZZ IN THE METAL COMMUNITY.
ROCK
LITA FORD
ANY 2 $5.00
TAKE 'EM!
MAN! WHO IS THIS?!
THIS IS LITA FORD'S NEW ONE. ISN'T IT HOT ?!?
KILL ME BABY...
YOU'RE DRESSED TO KILL
THE FOLLOW UP, "DANCIN' ON THE EDGE" IS ONE OF THE BEST ALBUMS OF THAT ERA, AND UNLIKE MOST MID-80'S METAL, STILL HOLDS UP TODAY. DESPITE A LACK OF PRESS, HARDCORE METAL HEADS ARE EXPOSED TO THE BLOND SIREN'S LETHAL LICKS.
SHE'S PLAYING NEXT WEEK WANNA GO?
HELL YEAH!

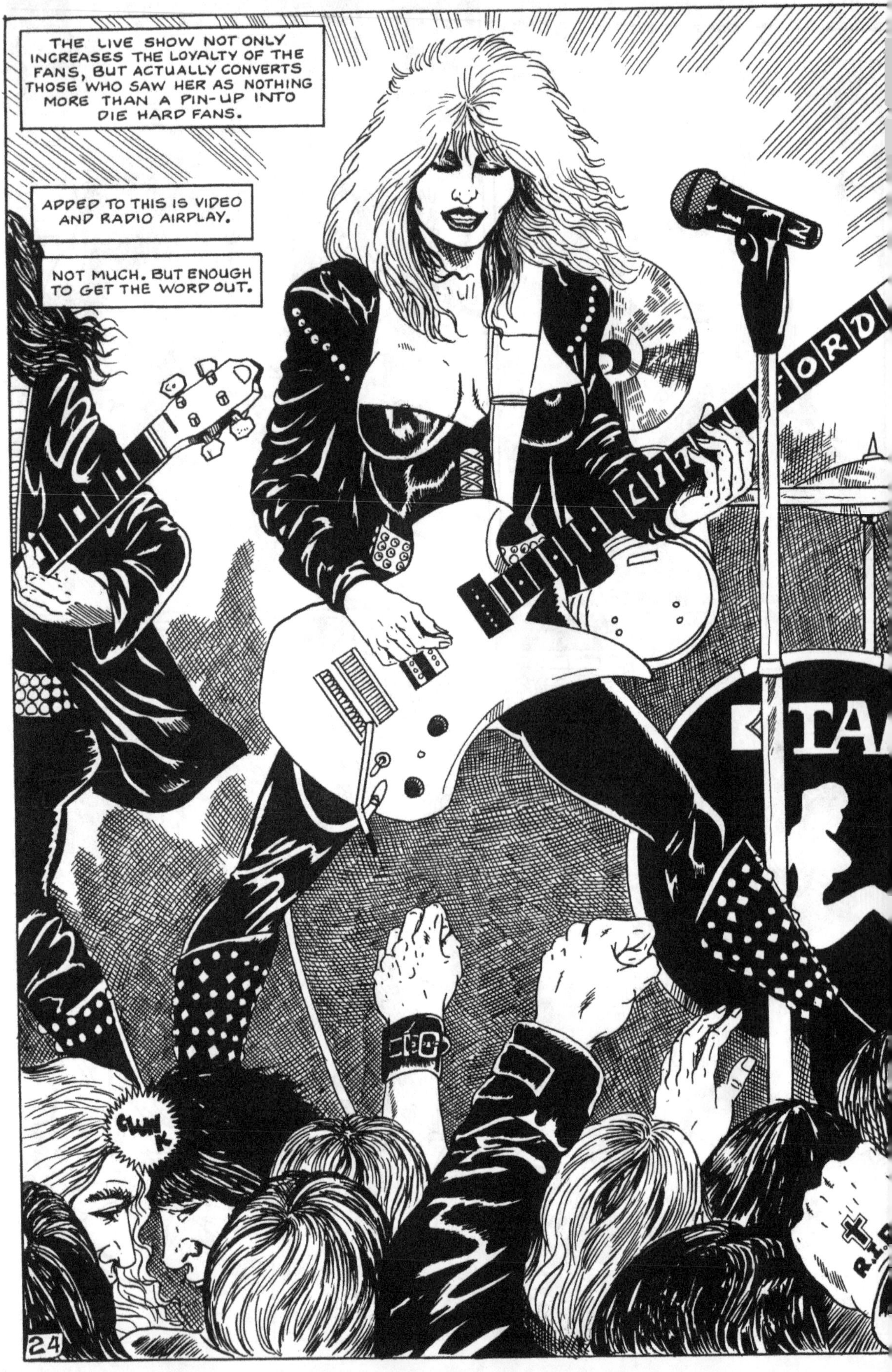
THE LIVE SHOW NOT ONLY INCREASES THE LOYALTY OF THE FANS, BUT ACTUALLY CONVERTS THOSE WHO SAW HER AS NOTHING MORE THAN A PIN-UP INTO DIE HARD FANS.
ADDED TO THIS IS VIDEO AND RADIO AIRPLAY.
NOT MUCH. BUT ENOUGH TO GET THE WORD OUT.
CLUNK

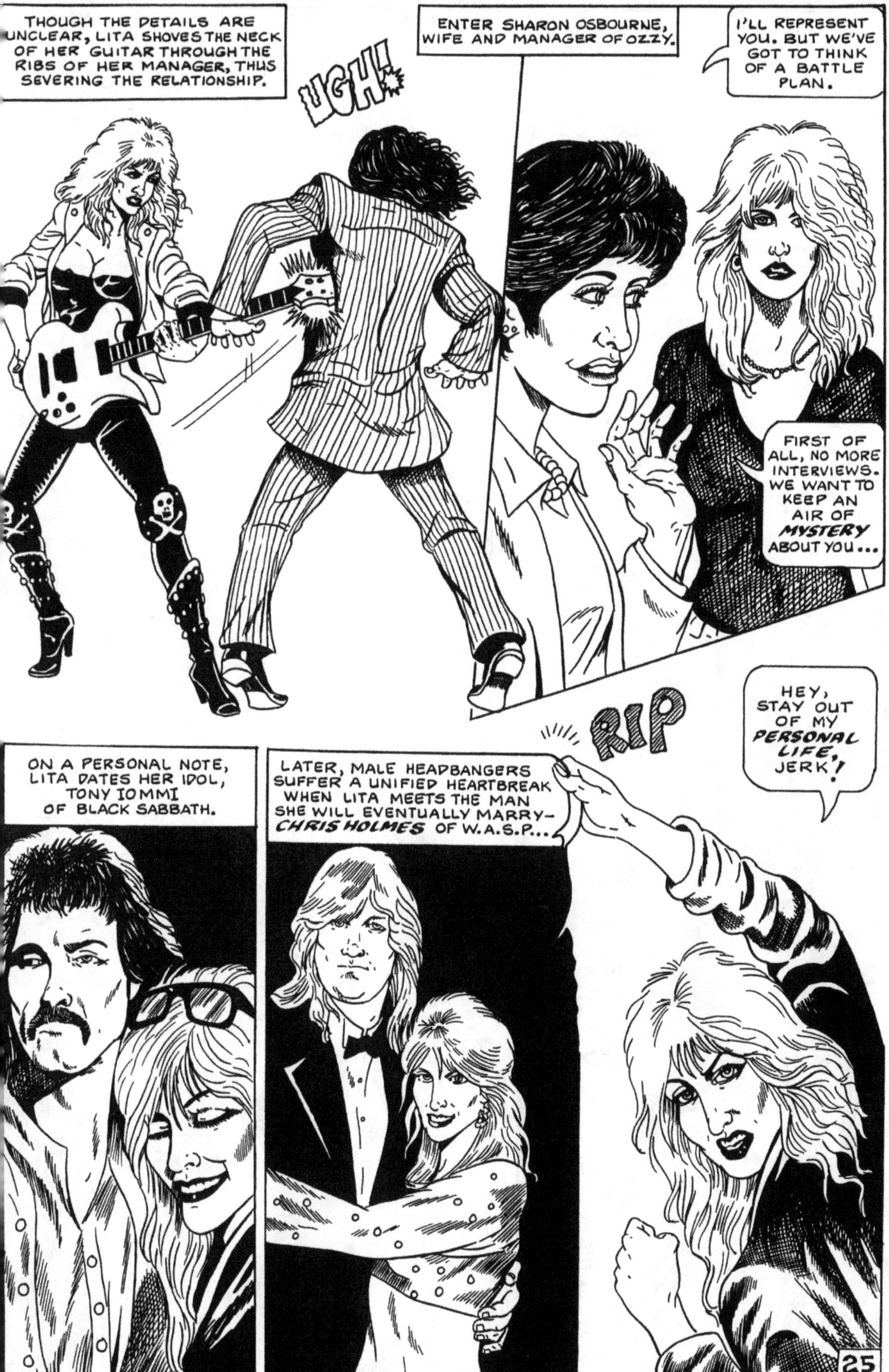

THOUGH THE DETAILS ARE UNCLEAR, LITA SHOVES THE NECK OF HER GUITAR THROUGH THE RIBS OF HER MANAGER, THUS SEVERING THE RELATIONSHIP.
UGH!
ENTER SHARON OSBOURNE, WIFE AND MANAGER OF OZZY.
I'LL REPRESENT YOU. BUT WE'VE GOT TO THINK OF A BATTLE PLAN.
FIRST OF ALL, NO MORE INTERVIEWS. WE WANT TO KEEP AN AIR OF MYSTERY ABOUT YOU...
ON A PERSONAL NOTE, LITA DATES HER IDOL, TONY IOMMI OF BLACK SABBATH.
LATER, MALE HEADBANGERS SUFFER A UNIFIED HEARTBREAK WHEN LITA MEETS THE MAN SHE WILL EVENTUALLY MARRY- CHRIS HOLMES OF W.A.S.P...
RIP
HEY, STAY OUT OF MY PERSONAL LIFE, JERK!

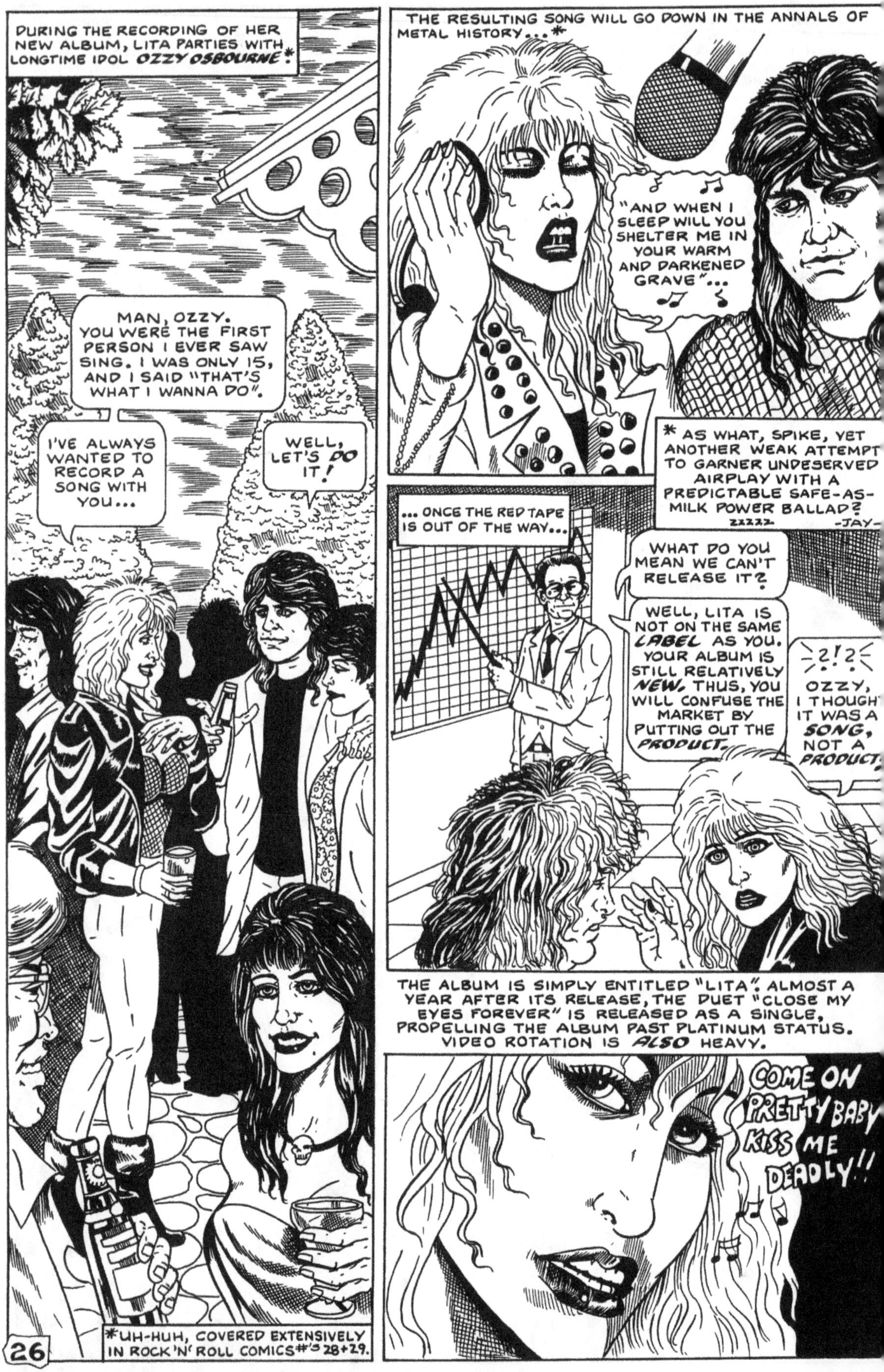
DURING THE RECORDING OF HER NEW ALBUM, LITA PARTIES WITH LONGTIME IDOL OZZY OSBOURNE*
MAN, OZZY. YOU WERE THE FIRST PERSON I EVER SAW SING. I WAS ONLY 15, AND I SAID "THAT'S WHAT I WANNA DO".
I'VE ALWAYS WANTED TO RECORD A SONG WITH YOU...
WELL, LET'S DO IT!
*UH-HUH, COVERED EXTENSIVELY IN ROCK 'N' ROLL COMICS #'S 28+29.
THE RESULTING SONG WILL GO DOWN IN THE ANNALS OF METAL HISTORY...*
"AND WHEN I SLEEP WILL YOU SHELTER ME IN YOUR WARM AND DARKENED GRAVE"...
* AS WHAT, SPIKE, YET ANOTHER WEAK ATTEMPT TO GARNER UNDESERVED AIRPLAY WITH A PREDICTABLE SAFE-AS-MILK POWER BALLAD? ZZZZZ -JAY-
... ONCE THE RED TAPE IS OUT OF THE WAY...
WHAT DO YOU MEAN WE CAN'T RELEASE IT?
WELL, LITA IS NOT ON THE SAME LABEL AS YOU. YOUR ALBUM IS STILL RELATIVELY NEW. THUS, YOU WILL CONFUSE THE MARKET BY PUTTING OUT THE PRODUCT.
?!?
OZZY, I THOUGHT IT WAS A SONG, NOT A PRODUCT.
THE ALBUM IS SIMPLY ENTITLED "LITA". ALMOST A YEAR AFTER ITS RELEASE, THE DUET "CLOSE MY EYES FOREVER" IS RELEASED AS A SINGLE, PROPELLING THE ALBUM PAST PLATINUM STATUS. VIDEO ROTATION IS ALSO HEAVY.
COME ON PRETTY BABY KISS ME DEADLY!!

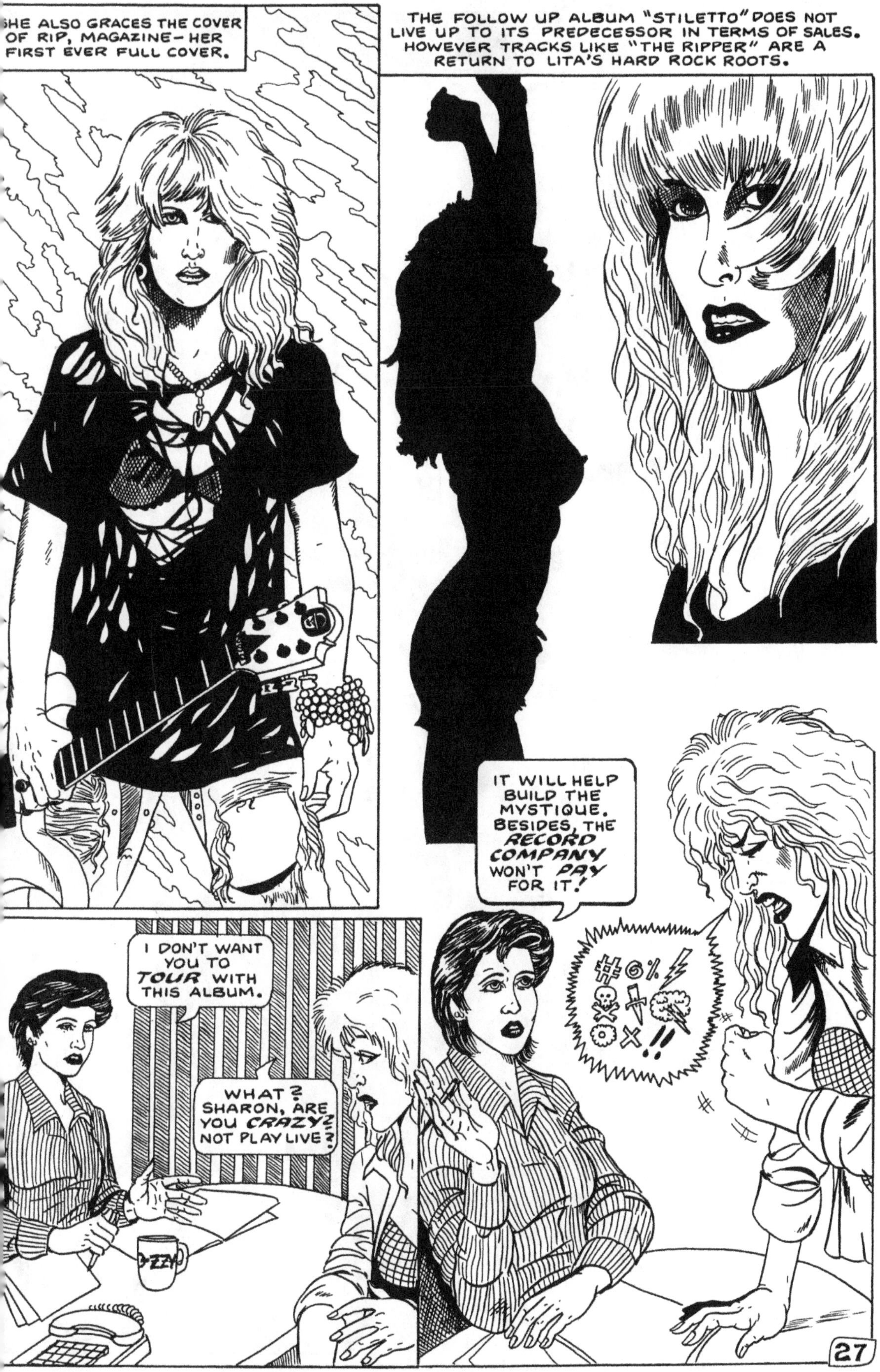
SHE ALSO GRACES THE COVER OF RIP, MAGAZINE—HER FIRST EVER FULL COVER.
THE FOLLOW UP ALBUM "STILETTO" DOES NOT LIVE UP TO ITS PREDECESSOR IN TERMS OF SALES. HOWEVER TRACKS LIKE "THE RIPPER" ARE A RETURN TO LITA'S HARD ROCK ROOTS.
I DON'T WANT YOU TO TOUR WITH THIS ALBUM.
WHAT? SHARON, ARE YOU CRAZY? NOT PLAY LIVE?
IT WILL HELP BUILD THE MYSTIQUE. BESIDES, THE RECORD COMPANY WON'T PAY FOR IT!

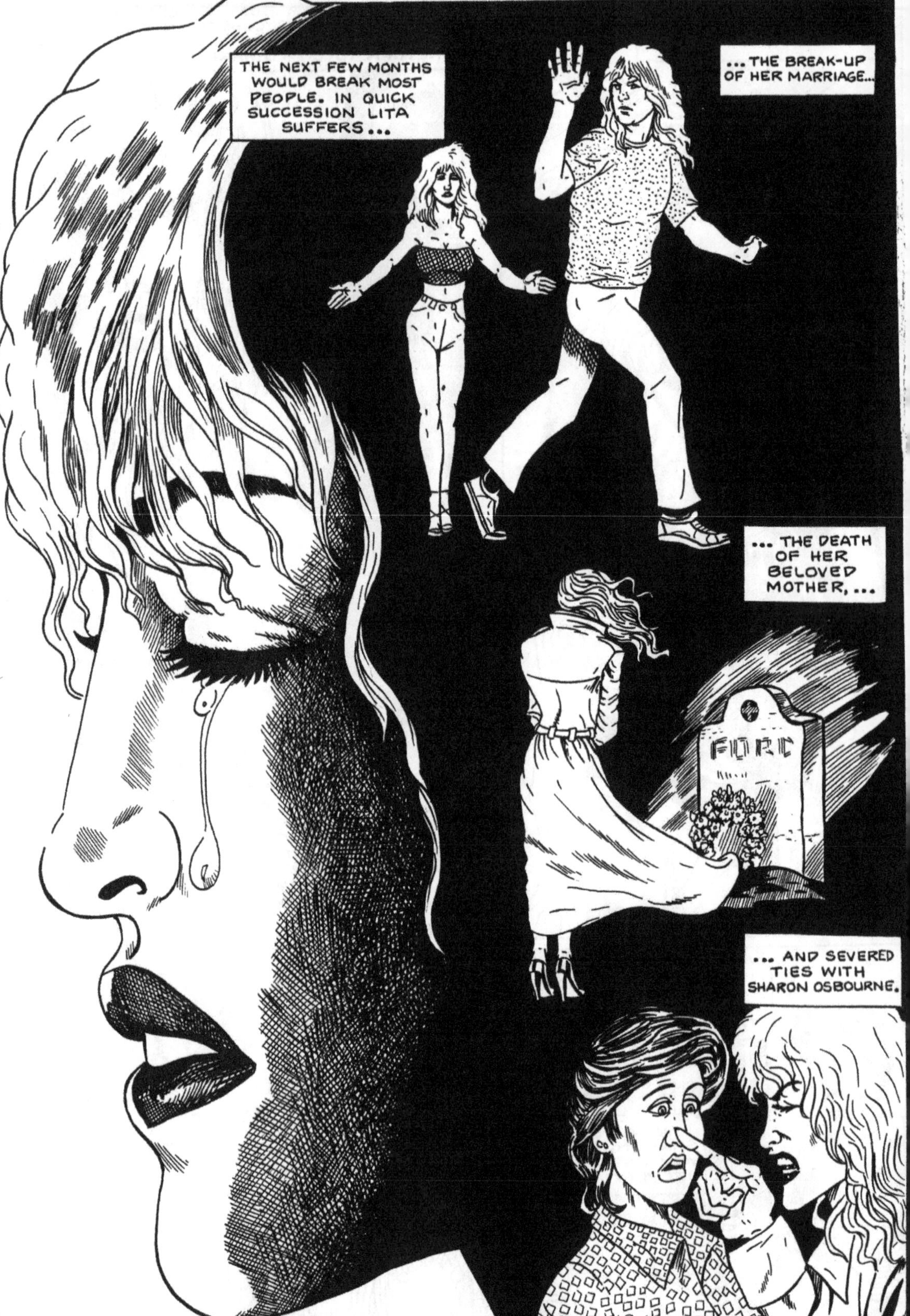
THE NEXT FEW MONTHS WOULD BREAK MOST PEOPLE. IN QUICK SUCCESSION LITA SUFFERS...
...THE BREAK-UP OF HER MARRIAGE...
... THE DEATH OF HER BELOVED MOTHER, ...
... AND SEVERED TIES WITH SHARON OSBOURNE.

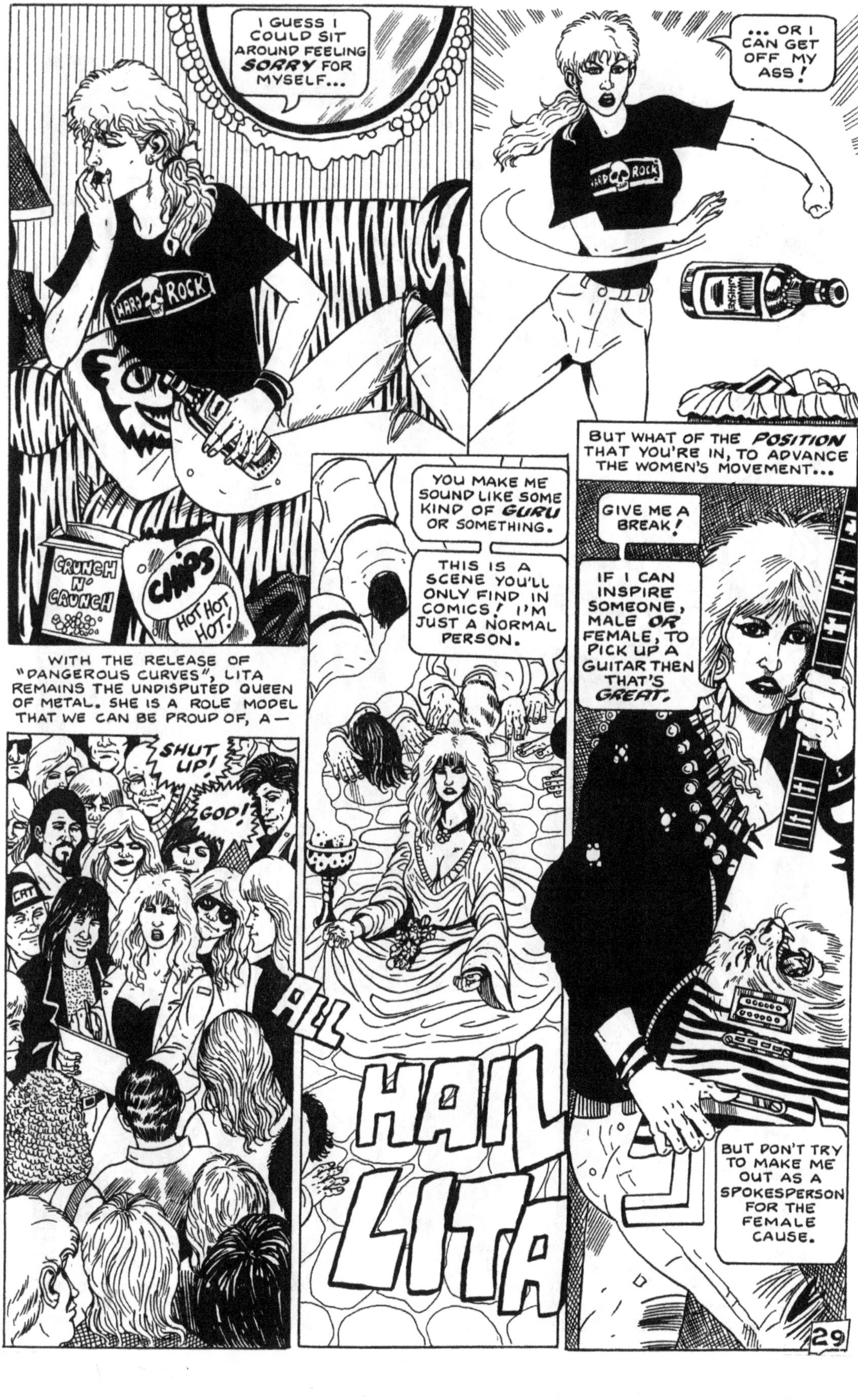
I GUESS I COULD SIT AROUND FEELING SORRY FOR MYSELF...
HARD ROCK
CRUNCH N' CRUNCH
CHIPS
HOT HOT HOT!
... OR I CAN GET OFF MY ASS!
HARD ROCK
WITH THE RELEASE OF "DANGEROUS CURVES", LITA REMAINS THE UNDISPUTED QUEEN OF METAL. SHE IS A ROLE MODEL THAT WE CAN BE PROUD OF, A—
SHUT UP!
GOD!
ALL HAIL LITA
YOU MAKE ME SOUND LIKE SOME KIND OF GURU OR SOMETHING.
THIS IS A SCENE YOU'LL ONLY FIND IN COMICS! I'M JUST A NORMAL PERSON.
BUT WHAT OF THE POSITION THAT YOU'RE IN, TO ADVANCE THE WOMEN'S MOVEMENT...
GIVE ME A BREAK!
IF I CAN INSPIRE SOMEONE, MALE OR FEMALE, TO PICK UP A GUITAR THEN THAT'S GREAT.
BUT DON'T TRY TO MAKE ME OUT AS A SPOKESPERSON FOR THE FEMALE CAUSE.

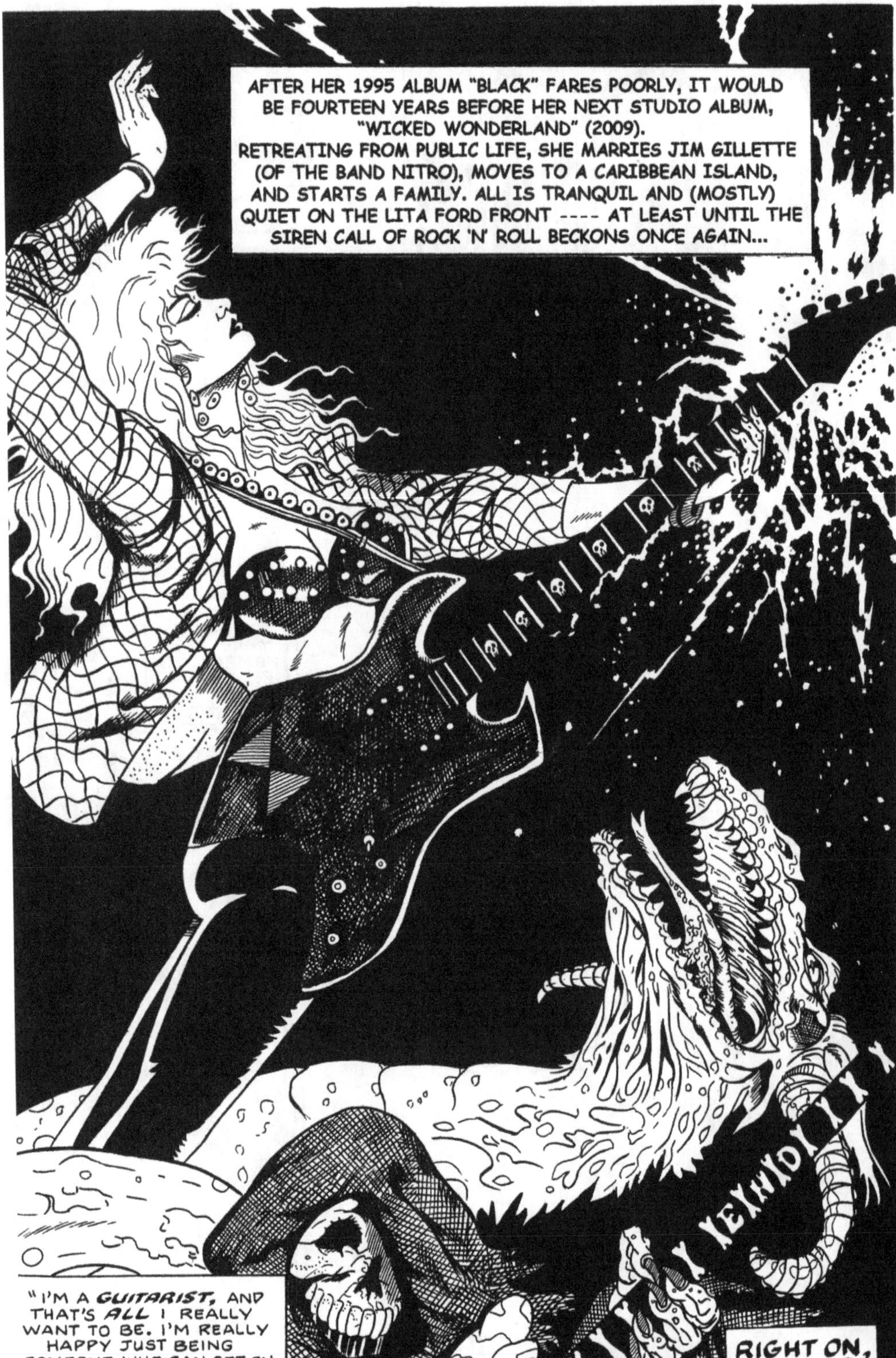
AFTER HER 1995 ALBUM "BLACK" FARES POORLY, IT WOULD BE FOURTEEN YEARS BEFORE HER NEXT STUDIO ALBUM, "WICKED WONDERLAND" (2009).
RETREATING FROM PUBLIC LIFE, SHE MARRIES JIM GILLETTE (OF THE BAND NITRO), MOVES TO A CARIBBEAN ISLAND, AND STARTS A FAMILY. ALL IS TRANQUIL AND (MOSTLY) QUIET ON THE LITA FORD FRONT ---- AT LEAST UNTIL THE SIREN CALL OF ROCK 'N' ROLL BECKONS ONCE AGAIN...
"I'M A GUITARIST, AND THAT'S ALL I REALLY WANT TO BE. I'M REALLY HAPPY JUST BEING SOMEONE WHO CAN GET ON STAGE, PLUG IN, AND KICK SOME SERIOUS ASS"!
RIGHT ON, LITA!
-END-

CPSIA information can be obtained
at www.ICGtesting.com
Printed in the USA
BVHW051514020321
601495BV00003B/298

9 781948 216227

#ERASEHATE WITH THE MATTHEW SHEPARD FOUNDATION

With your donated dollars and volunteer hours, we work tirelessly to erase hate from every corner of America through our programs.

SPEAKING ENGAGEMENTS

Since Matt's death in 1998, Judy and Dennis have been determined to prevent others from similar tragedies. By sharing their story, they are able to carry on Matt's legacy.

HATE CRIMES REPORTING

Our work to improve reporting includes conducting trainings for law enforcement agencies, building relationships between community leaders and law enforcement, and developing policy reform in reporting practices.

LARAMIE PROJECT

MSF offers support to productions of The Laramie Project, which depicts the events leading up to and after Matt's murder. It remains one of the most performed plays in America.

MATTHEW'S PLACE

MatthewsPlace.com is a blog designed to provide young LGBTQ+ people with an outlet for their voices. From finance to health to love and dating, and everything in between, our writers contribute excellent material.

Erase Hate

Matthew Shepard Foundation
embracing diversity